WEEK LOAN

Remember to return on time **or** renew at
https://icity.bcu.ac.uk/ or
http://capitadiscovery.co.uk/bcu/account
Items in demand may not be renewable

Orders: Please contact How2become Ltd, Suite 3, 50 Churchill Square Business Centre, Kings Hill, Kent ME19 4YU. You can also order via the e mail address info@how2become.co.uk.

ISBN: 9781910202098

First published in 2014 by How2Become Ltd

Typeset for How2become Ltd by gnibel.com

Printed in Great Britain for How2become Ltd
by CMP (uk) Limited, Poole, Dorset.

CONTENTS

INTRODUCTION

Welcome to the insider's guide to becoming a paramedic. This guide has been designed to help you prepare for the Paramedic/Emergency Care Assistant selection process.

The author of this guide, Richard McMunn, spent over 16 years in the emergency services attending many incidents including road traffic collisions, where he would work alongside paramedic's and emergency care assistants. He also sat on numerous interview panels assessing potential candidates to join the job and knows what calibre of person it takes to succeed. You will find his advice invaluable and inspiring in your pursuit to joining what is probably one of the most exciting careers available.

Whilst the selection process to join the Ambulance Service is highly competitive and jobs are few and far between, there are a number of things you can do in order to improve your chances of success, and they are all contained within this guide.

The book has been split up into useful sections to make it easier for you to prepare for each stage. Read each section

carefully and take notes as you progress. Don't ever give up on your dreams; if you really want to become a paramedic or emergency care assistant, then you can do it.

The way to prepare for selection is to embark on a programme of in-depth preparation, and this guide will show you exactly how to do just that.

If you need any help with motivation, getting fit or further paramedic interview help and advice, then we offer a wide range of products to assist you. These are all available through our online shop www.how2become.com.

We also run a 1-day intensive Paramedic Course. Details are available at the website www.ParamedicCourse.co.uk.

Once again, thank you for your custom and we wish you every success in your pursuit to becoming a paramedic.

Work hard, stay focused and be what you want…

Best wishes,

The how2become team

The How2become Team

PREFACE BY AUTHOR RICHARD McMUNN

During my time in the Fire Service I had the chance to meet and work with many paramedics and emergency care assistants (ECA's). Every single one of them was a true professional and they always took tremendous pride in their work. I attended many road traffic collisions, house fires and rail accidents in my time, and more often than not I was required to work alongside these brave men and women. Not once did they fail in their duty to provide a high level of care to those people who needed them most.

Whilst in the Fire Service I also managed to speak to many different people who were directly involved in the recruitment process for joining the Ambulance Service, and I was also fortunate enough to enjoy a day riding with an ambulance crew attending many different operational incidents. Having asked a number of them what it takes to pass the selection process, one word kept constantly coming up – **preparation**.

I have always been a great believer in preparation. Preparation was my key to success and it is also yours. Without the right

level of preparation you will be setting out on the route to failure. The Ambulance Service is very hard to join, but if you follow the steps that I have compiled within this guide then you will increase your chances of success dramatically.

Remember, you are learning how to be a successful candidate, not a successful paramedic.

Before you apply to join the Ambulance Service, you need to be fully confident that you too are capable of providing a high level of service. If you think you can do it, and you can rise to the challenge, then you just might be the type of person the Ambulance Service is looking for.

As you progress through this guide you will notice that the qualities required to be a paramedic are a common theme. You must learn these qualities, and also be able to demonstrate throughout the selection process that you can meet them, if you are to have any chance of successfully passing the selection process.

As with any guide that I write, or training course that I run, I always focus the student's mind on the qualities that are required to carry out a specific job competently. More often than not, recruiters will assess you against these qualities during the selection process and therefore you must concentrate your preparation on this area.

Direct entry into the Ambulance Service as an apprentice paramedic is rare; therefore, I have aimed this guide at those people who are applying to university and also those people applying through the direct entry route. Regardless of your chosen entry route, please take the time to read the entire guide.

CHAPTER ONE

ABOUT THE AMBULANCE SERVICE

Before we start to look into the selection process and more importantly how you can increase your chances of success, we will first of all need to take a look at the Ambulance Service and also the role of a paramedic. It is important to point out at this stage that although the guide makes reference to the paramedic selection process, it is also highly suitable for those people who are applying to become an emergency care assistant.

The first stage of any job preparation is to study the organisation that you are applying to join and also the role that you are applying for. There is a very good reason for this. The vast majority of recruitment teams will focus their assessment of candidates on how best they suit the job description, person specification and the general requirements of the role. If you are applying via the university route then you should still familiarise yourself with the role of the ambulance service and a paramedic.

To begin with let's take a look at the Ambulance Service, its role and most importantly its core values.

OVERVIEW

The Ambulance Service in the UK is under the authority of the National Health Service (NHS) and is divided into separate NHS Ambulance Trusts covering different geographical areas. The size of the geographical area will vary and you will notice during your research that a number of trusts have amalgamated into larger areas. This will have very little impact on you as an applicant but it is still important that you are aware of the structure and geographical area of the trust you are applying to join.

THE ROLE OF THE AMBULANCE SERVICE

Most people believe that the Ambulance Service is simply there to respond to emergency incidents such as road traffic collisions (RTCs), seriously ill or injured patients, fires and other such incidents. Whilst these are the core roles that the service undertakes, there are also a number of other important duties that are carried out, such as patient transport services. These are the employees of the Ambulance Service who carry disabled, elderly and vulnerable people to and from outpatient appointments, hospital admissions and also day centres and clinics.

Behind the operational ambulance crew is a team of people who have different roles, all designed to provide the necessary support required that is so valued by the community. To begin with, there are the 999 call operators who take the initial calls. Their job is to gather as much information as possible about the emergency call, the nature of the incident, its location

and the level of response that is required. These people are integral to the Ambulance Service and are crucial to patient care. For example, if a patient is critically ill they may need to talk the caller through a lifesaving procedure whilst they wait for the ambulance crews to get there.

In addition to paramedics and those who provide frontline support, there are also a number of other different roles within the Ambulance Service. As an example, there are over 4000 people employed by the London Ambulance Service alone!

A TYPICAL AMBULANCE SERVICE – THE LONDON AMBULANCE SERVICE

The London Ambulance Service NHS Trust is the largest free Ambulance Service in the world and is twice as busy as any other Ambulance Service in the UK. From its headquarters and central control in Waterloo, the biggest in Europe, it answers over 3,000 emergency calls a day from the culturally diverse seven million people of Greater London, an area of 620 square miles covered by 70 ambulance stations.

Frontline ambulance crews provide cover 24-hours a day, 365 days a year, and respond to all emergency 999 calls made to the service. Most crew members are paramedics and emergency care assistants, who combine their medical training with advanced driving skills in order to provide a rapid response.

Ambulance crews are made up of either two emergency care assistants, or one emergency care assistant and a paramedic who share the driving duties during a shift. All ambulance drivers are bound by the Highway Code, so the job requires a high level of skill to negotiate the heavily congested roads of London quickly but safely.

When calls are received at Central Ambulance Control, they are categorised according to the severity of the illness or injury. The calls are then dispatched to the crews by a classification system (sample only):

- Category A (immediately life-threatening)
- Category C (not serious or life-threatening)

This priority dispatch system means ambulances and additional resources, such as the rapid response units; reach the most critical patients first.

GENERAL REQUIREMENTS FOR JOINING THE AMBULANCE SERVICE

Applicants wishing to enter the Ambulance Service will normally need to be over 18 (21 in some areas), be physically fit, hold a clean driving licence and be able to pass a series of entrance exams. The entry criteria for each role will vary depending on the service you are applying to join. In addition to the job of a paramedic, there are also other support roles available such as:

- Ambulance care assistant
- Emergency care assistant
- Emergency care practitioner
- Emergency medical dispatcher
- Patient Transport Services controller

Educational requirements vary but most services require candidates to hold at least four GCSEs at grades A-C or suitable alternatives. All applicants must pass a medical examination and a police/criminal records check, as staff will have substantial access to children and vulnerable persons.

However, each Ambulance Service sets its own entry requirements and there may be regional variations in what is acceptable, therefore it is advisable to contact the individual NHS Ambulance Trust directly for further information on what is required. There will also be set requirements that relate to driving qualifications and these form part of the essential criteria for the role.

PARAMEDIC SCIENCE DEGREE ROUTES INTO THE AMBULANCE SERVICE

More and more NHS Trusts are now requiring paramedic applicants to hold a Paramedic Science Degree, and as such, the direct entry route is becoming less available. We will cover the Paramedic Science Degree route within this guide but please check with the NHS Trust you wish to join for more details about their specific entry requirements.

DIRECT ENTRY AS AN APPRENTICE PARAMEDIC

There may also be the option to join the Ambulance Service as an apprentice paramedic. For example, at the time of writing the London Ambulance Service currently operate this entry option.

ENTRY REQUIREMENTS

Entry requirements for student paramedic positions will vary, depending upon the employer. The range of paramedic science courses at university varies in terms of entry requirements but a minimum of 5 GCSEs (including English, mathematics and/or a science) plus at least 2 A' levels or equivalent qualifications is typically needed. However, it is essential that

you contact each university directly for information on their admissions policy and entry requirements. You'll also need a full, manual driving licence. Ambulance services use vehicles of different gross weights and staff will be required to hold a driving licence with the appropriate classifications.

In some ambulance services, a 'standard' driving licence may be acceptable, but if you passed your test after 1996, you will need an additional qualification to drive larger vehicles and carry passengers. Some employers may provide support for staff who need to gain further licence classifications, but this is not standard across the UK. It is therefore essential that applicants check with each ambulance service trust to which they intend to apply.

TRAINING

To practice as a paramedic, you must be registered with the Health and Care Professions Council (HCPC). In order to register with the HCPC, you must successfully complete an HCPC-approved programme in paramedic science. A number of universities have been approved by the HCPC to run programmes leading to a diploma, foundation degree and/or BSc honours degree in paramedic science. Additionally some ambulance service trusts are approved by the HCPC to provide training for the Institute of Healthcare Development (IHCD) paramedic award, leading to registration.

Courses tend to be modular with flexible entry and exit points, depending upon your academic qualifications and any relevant experience. They last from two to five years, depending on whether you study full or part time. It's important to check entry requirements with the university concerned and with the ambulance service trust/s in the areas where you want to work.

Training comprises both theory and practical clinical experience, including several weeks in various hospital departments. Much of the training of paramedics is carried out under the supervision of senior doctors.

APPLYING FOR PARAMEDIC TRAINING

Students applying for full-time university courses usually need to apply through the Universities and Colleges Admissions Service (UCAS). Those already working as student paramedics (or qualified ambulance technicians where these posts still exist) should speak to their employing ambulance service about applications for part-time courses.

CHAPTER TWO
THE ROLE OF THE PARAMEDIC

Within this section of the guide I have provided you with generic details about the roles of a paramedic and an emergency care assistant. It is important that you fully understand the role that you are applying for; as you will need to be able to match you own skills and experiences with the requirements of the role. The first stage in your pursuit to becoming a paramedic or emergency care assistant is to fully learn and understand the role – this is crucial to your success.

PARAMEDIC JOB SUMMARY

Paramedics are usually the first senior healthcare professional at an incident or medical emergency. The types of incident that they attend vary greatly but can involve road traffic collisions (RTCs), fires, rail accidents and seriously injured or ill patients. Paramedics usually work on their own or with a technician or emergency care assistant, with whom they will assess the needs of the patient and provide the appropriate

treatment or care. They will also keep the local hospital informed of the condition of the patient so that they can prepare for their arrival.

As a paramedic you will be required to use high-tech equipment, such as defibrillators, spinal and traction splints and intravenous drips, and you will also be required to administer oxygen and drugs. As you can imagine it is a highly specialised role which requires a unique set of abilities.

Some of the more common requirements of the role include:

1. Ensure personal and/or vehicle readiness at all times and be available to attend emergency and non-emergency incidents. Maintaining communication with your control centre to inform them of your exact location and movements. These updates will also include details of personnel with whom you are working and they will allow the central control to dispatch resources as and when required.

2. Conducting patient assessments at emergency incidents, including interpretation of 12-lead ECG when appropriate. Once the assessment of the patient has been carried out, you will then be required to administer the appropriate level of patient care in accordance with your operating manuals and procedures.

3. Complete and maintain a full and accurate clinical record for all of your patients. In particular this will include details of:

    *   Your observations of the patient;
    *   The type of treatment given;
    *   Drug administration;
    *   Final destination of the patient.

4. Deal with the relatives of the patient, where appropriate using effective communication. This in particular requires you to have competent 'people skills'.

5. Carry out first responder duties and conduct specialist patient assessment and treatment at the scene of an operational incident.

6. Liaise with other health professionals and communicate complex information to all levels both internally and externally.

7. Interact with, persuade and reassure extremely distressed, emotional or mentally disturbed persons.

8. Work with other members of the Emergency Services in order to carry out patient care. For example, whilst attending road traffic collisions you will need to liaise and communicate with the Fire Service in order to carefully and successfully extricate casualties from the wreckage.

EMERGENCY CARE ASSISTANT JOB SUMMARY

Emergency care assistants respond to 999 calls as part of an accident and emergency crew. They usually work under the direction of a paramedic. Part of this role includes the need to drive emergency vehicles as directed by the ambulance service whilst under blue light conditions. It will be your responsibility to carry out thorough checks on both your vehicle and your equipment.

Some of the more common duties that an emergency care assistant is required to perform will include:

1. Drive ambulance service vehicles as required including responding to emergency incidents and also patient transport duties (PTS).

 how2become

2.   Maintain all vehicles and equipment in a clean and serviceable condition.

3.   Carry out regular checks on your vehicle so that it is ready for immediate dispatch. This will include oil, water and fuel levels, tyres, batteries etc.

4.   Carry out daily checks on all of your equipment so that it is serviceable and fully operational at all times.

5.   Carry out a handover at change of shift and complete any required tasks or duties. It will be crucial that you inform your work colleagues of any equipment defects or any equipment that has taken out of service.

6.   Carry emergency patients either as a driver or attendant.

7.   Carry out radio procedures with control room staff and keep an accurate log.

8.   Keep all of your paperwork and documentation up to date, including the station logbook, accident report forms, deficiency lists, time sheets and telephone accounts.

9.   Carry out all of your work in accordance with service orders and instructions.

CHAPTER THREE

TRAINING TO BECOME
A PARAMEDIC/EMERGENCY CARE
ASSISTANT

In this section of the guide I will provide you with details of how to train as a paramedic. To begin with, let's take a look at direct entry and training.

TRAINING VIA THE STUDENT/APPRENTICE PARAMEDIC TRAINING COURSE (SAMPLE ONLY)

You'll train to be a paramedic over five years. Your training will be split into modules and combine lessons with practical placements and workshops, so knowledge gained in the classroom can be put into practice on the road.

The course covers everything from driving an ambulance to advanced patient assessments. Successful candidates will complete an introductory course of nine weeks, which

includes three weeks' driver training. During this time you will cover the theoretical and practical skills elements which will allow you to undertake duties on an emergency ambulance with a paramedic.

Once candidates have successfully completed their consolidation period, they will work alongside a paramedic as a paramedic apprentice – working 37.5 hours per week averaged over a 12-week rota, covering 24 hours, seven days per week, 365 days per year.

Apprentices will complete a Foundation Year (year 0) during which they will be required to complete an access to study module, as well as ongoing assessments in practice of their clinical and communication skills and attitudes and behaviours. Those who successfully reach the standards required in practice, and complete the access module, will be registered for the Foundation Degree in Paramedic Science in September/October.

The Foundation Degree runs over a four-year period, on a part-time basis. This is mainly on a distance study mode with clinical placements to consolidate learning and develop specific practice competencies; clinical placements will take place in both an ambulance and non-ambulance context.

Students should be aware that the course equates to 240 academic credits – 120 at level 4 and 120 at level 5 – and that every credit requires a minimum of 10 hours of student effort. Although time required to complete study will vary, students should be aware that between seven and 16 hours study will be required by the average student per week in their own time.

Through the course, you will have the opportunity to develop knowledge, skills and competencies that underpin practice across the paramedic science field. The approach

of the degree is inter-disciplinary, with opportunities for specialisation where appropriate.

The qualification is attuned to the NHS modernisation agenda, the Knowledge and Skills Framework and the Health and Care Professions Council's (HCPC) standards of proficiency. The Foundation Degree in Paramedic Sciences has been approved by the HCPC, which means that on successful completion of the award you will be eligible to apply to the HCPC for professional registration as a paramedic.

Application forms can normally be obtained either by visiting the website of the relevant NHS trust you wish to join, or by telephoning the recruitment line. You will find that many NHS trusts don't recruit that often so it is important that you keep monitoring their website for recruitment updates – you do not want to miss a recruitment opportunity!

The application form must be completed in full; CVs are usually not accepted. The 'Personal Details' section is relatively straightforward to complete. Perhaps the two most important sections of the application form are those relating to the 'Reasons for Applying for this Post' and 'Experience and Personal Skills'. If these sections are not answered satisfactorily then this will result in a failure to be short-listed for the interview. It is important that you read the 'person specification' for the role you are applying for prior to completing this part of the application form.

When responding to these types of question you should provide details of your experience and training to explain why you are suitable for this post. When describing your current or previous work experience, you should specify your responsibilities, rather than those of your department or team.

Address all the criteria on the person specification, showing how you meet each one. You should mention experience,

skills, achievements and knowledge gained, not only in past employment, but also through other activities such as voluntary or community work, experience in the home, and leisure interests. You should, where possible, give examples of specific situations that you have come across and how you have dealt with the situation and the people involved.

Within the 'Application Form' section of this guide I have provided you with essential advice on how to answer the questions contained within your application form.

TRAINING VIA THE PARAMEDIC SCIENCE DEGREE ROUTE (SAMPLE ONLY)

In order to obtain an application form for the Paramedic Science Degree route you will need to apply directly to the university of your choice and have a good standard of education. This is generally five GCSEs at grade C or above (including maths, English and a science) or equivalent.

You will also need:

- 120 CATS points (equivalent to one A-level) for entry onto the Foundation Degree programme.

- 360 CATS points (equivalent to three A-levels) for entry onto the BSc Hons programme.

If you are a mature student, then equivalent qualifications and experience will be considered.

You will also need to have a full manual UK driving licence, driving experience, meet their driving licence criteria with regards to points and hold provisional C1 on your licence – this may vary depending on the course so please check with your chosen university for more details.

EXAMPLES OF UNIVERSITY COURSES
IN THE SOUTH EAST REGION

Full-time courses:

- **University of Hertfordshire BSc (Hons)**
  This degree runs over three academic years. On completion of the course you will attain a BSc (Hons) in Paramedic Science and will be eligible to register with the Health and Care Professions Council (HCPC) as a paramedic.

- **University of Hertfordshire Foundation Degree (FdSc)**
  This programme includes a high percentage of taught sessions supported by e-learning and practical placements. It runs over two academic years and on completion you will attain a Foundation Degree in Paramedic Science and will be eligible to register with the Health and Care Professions Council (HCPC) as a paramedic.

- **University of Greenwich BSc (Hons)**
  This degree runs over three academic years. On completion of the course you will attain a BSc (Hons) in Paramedic Science and will be eligible to register with the Health and Care Professions Council (HCPC) as a paramedic.

- **St George's, University of London Foundation Degree (FdSc)**
  This programme primarily involves e-learning, supported by a number of taught sessions and practical placements. The programme runs over two academic years and on completion you will attain a Foundation Degree in Paramedic Science and will be eligible to register with the Health and Care Professions Council (HCPC) as a paramedic.

 how2become

THE WRITTEN TESTS AND ASSESSMENTS

In order to be accepted onto some Paramedic Science Degree programmes you may have to sit a Maths test, a Literacy test or both. You may also be required to sit a series of tests if you are applying to join via the direct student/apprentice paramedic route. The tests will vary from trust to trust but there is usually a multi-choice type numeracy test with a tick box answer sheet and a verbal comprehension test where you have to read a passage then answer questions on it. This is sometimes followed by a map reading exercise to test your reasoning ability.

Within this guide I have provided you with different sections relating to the tests in order to help you during your preparation. Please make sure you confirm the type of tests you are required to sit for the NHS trust you are applying to join before using them, as not all of them will be relevant to your chosen entry route.

FITNESS TESTS

Once again, each NHS trust will vary in the type of tests you have to undertake. You may also be required to undertake a fitness assessment before you are permitted to enrol on the Paramedic Science Degree.

An example of this type of test is where you will be required to pair up with another candidate and carry a 48kg dummy placed in a carry chair up and down a short flight of stairs. You must ensure that you utilise correct lifting techniques, i.e. back straight, look up and bend knees etc. This will also demonstrate your grip and overall body strength. An instructor will demonstrate the techniques involved before you are requested to perform the lift and carry.

Some NHS trusts will ask you to perform a variety of different tests including a step test, cardiac massage test and lifting test, which are all designed to assess your ability to carry out the demanding tasks of the role.

THE INTERVIEW

Successful completion of all of the preceding stages of the selection process will result in a formal interview.

You should prepare for the interview by finding out as much as possible about the particular Ambulance Service you are hoping to join and the role that you are applying for. The section within this guide that relates to the interview will provide you with lots of useful information that will help you prepare and pass the paramedic interview. This can be enhanced by contacting the duty station officer at your local Ambulance Station and trying to arrange a 'ride out' with an experienced crew. If the NHS trust does not offer this facility then I still advise that you try to visit your local ambulance station in order to speak to the crews about their role and what it involves.

If you do manage to obtain permission for a 'ride-out', you will be required to complete a form that includes a disclaimer. Then you will be required to arrange a short term temporary Personal Liability Insurance through your insurance broker. You will have to produce the cover note before commencing the 'ride out'. This is an excellent method of finding out about the role that you are applying for and will assist with your answers at interview.

Please see the 'INTERVIEW' section of your guide for more advice relating to the formal interview procedure and how to prepare.

THE DRIVING TEST

The driving assessment usually consists of a pre-driving check, a familiarisation drive, a test drive and an oral Highway Code Assessment.

This will be conducted to Department of Transport requirements and your driving will be assessed in a manual, minibus-sized vehicle. You will be asked to drive around an area to demonstrate your ability to drive a large vehicle and reverse into a marked parking bay. You must take your driving licence to the test with you and if you possess the new kind of credit card style licence you must take along the paper attachment issued with the licence. If you wear glasses for reading and/or driving you must take them with you too.

Failure to take your licence and glasses will result in the cancellation of your test.

THE HEALTH ASSESSMENT/MEDICAL

You will be asked to take with you a completed health questionnaire, which will be sent to you with the instructions to attend.

Once again you must take with you any glasses that you normally wear for driving and/or reading as the assessment will include an eye test. You will also be requested to take one form of photographic ID (i.e. passport or photo card driving licence), this is to make sure that the applicant already interviewed is attending in person. Your height-to-weight ratio and your general state of health will be checked.

You will be required to provide a urine sample during the assessment so make sure you are able to do so. The medical assessment will also involve testing for hepatitis B and C.

C1 DRIVING LICENSE

You will find that the vast majority of Paramedic Science Degree University courses and NHS trusts now require you to have C1 on your driving license, whether that is provisional or full.

The C1 driving license category allows you to drive vehicles between 3500kg and 7500kg and a trailer up to 750kg. You need to be 18 years old and hold a full manual licence to apply. It is required by many trusts because the weight of some of the vehicles is over 3500kg. Your first step will be to apply for a provisional license from the DVLA.

HOW TO OBTAIN A C1 PROVISIONAL LICENSE

In order to obtain your provisional C1 you need to get a 'D1 application form' from the DVLA or your local post office. You will be required to fill in the form and also under go a health check from your GP. You will need to phone your GP and arrange the health check yourself, usually at your own expense. If your GP is with the same trust that as the ambulance service you are applying for then they may carry out this for free.

Once you have completed the form and your health check has been carried out you must then send the forms off to the DVLA. You will normally receive your provisional after a few weeks.

THE THEORY TESTS

In order to successfully gain your C1 driving license you will need to take two tests. The test is split into two parts. The first test is a multiple choice question paper, for which you will

need to learn about Light Goods Vehicles. This will include tacographs, road signs, first aid and general questions that are similar to your car theory test. The next part is a hazard perception test. During this test you will be required to watch 14 clips and pick up the potential hazards which could pose a risk to you or other road users. It is exactly the same test used for the manual license.

Once you have successfully passed the theory test element you will need to find a training school who will teach you what is required to pass the practical test. It is recommended that you carry out an intensive course at a suitably qualified training centre. These courses vary in price and they will normally last between 5 and 7 days, with a test at the end of it. Alternatively you may decide to choose individual lessons and these will probably last about 3 hours per session.

THE C1 DRIVING TEST

The test consists of 3 parts. During the first part of the test the examiner will ask you a number of questions based around safety. These could be anything ranging from routine daily checks of the vehicle, to loading. Your instructor will have gone over these with you during you training.

The next part is a 'control exercise' and will form two parts. The first involves you having to reverse the vehicle into a bay. This is made up of several stages, including being able to stop on a line, reverse around a cone and make it into the box parking space without going over the rear line.

The second part of the control exercise is a controlled stop. You will be asked to reach speeds of up to 20 miles per hour and then stop in a controlled manor between 2 cones.

After this element of the test is completed you will be

assessed on your driving skills during a 40 minute drive. You are only allowed to make 15 minor errors and you are not allowed any serious ones.

Once you have successfully passed the test then you will have your licence sent off to the DVLA for you by the assessor. You will receive the new licence with your C1 category added soon after.

Now let's take a look at my top 10 insider tips for success.

CHAPTER FOUR

MY TOP 10 INSIDER TIPS AND ADVICE

During my life I have attended many different interviews, career assessments and selection processes. I estimate that I have been successful at over 90% of them and I put that success down to the in-depth preparation strategies that I follow, prior to the application stage. Over the next few pages I will provide you with a number of important 'insider tips' that will allow you to prepare for, and pass, the selection process for becoming a paramedic or emergency care assistant. Although some of them may appear obvious, do not ignore them!

INSIDER TIP NUMBER 1 – UNDERSTAND HOW TO COMPLETE THE APPLICATION FORM

This may sound obvious but you will be surprised at how many people fail to complete the application form correctly.

Most of the sections contained within the application form are relatively straightforward to complete. However, the section relating to the reasons why you want to join, and what experiences you have to match the job description, catches most people out. These questions need a focused response that relates both to the 'person specification' and the vision/ values of the Ambulance Service you are applying to join.

When you sit down to complete the application form, you must ensure that you have a copy of the person specification/ job description next to you. It is crucial that you try to cross-match your skills and experiences with them, as the assessor, or person who is scoring your form, will use these as a basis for marking your form. Too many people spend very little time on the application form and as a result they end up failing. Remember that there will be literally hundreds of people applying for just one job so your form needs to stand out for the right reasons.

Another area in which applicants fall down is an inability to follow simple instructions. If you fail to complete the form in the correct colour ink then this can lead to failure. Make sure you read the form very carefully before you complete it and remember to photocopy your completed form before sending it off by recorded delivery. There is a strong possibility that you will be asked questions relating to your form during the interview stage. If you are required to complete an online application, be sure to check your grammar and spelling before clicking the SUBMIT button as you will lose marks for any errors made.

Within this guide I have dedicated an entire section to the application form and I have also provided you with actual successful responses to help you structure your own. Treat the application form very seriously and make sure you take

time when creating your responses. If you don't create an adequate response you will not progress to the assessment centre or the proceeding stages.

INSIDER TIP NUMBER 2 –
MAKE SURE YOU ARE FIT TO WORK

The very nature of the paramedic's work involves heavy lifting and repetitive cardiac massage work. Whilst you will not be required to perform these duties every day of your career, you do need to be ready to perform them adequately when the need arises.

Climbing steep stairs, lifting patients and working long and unpredictable hours are all trademarks of the paramedic profession and you must be prepared for this. During the selection process you may have to undergo some form of physical assessment and you will certainly have to undergo a medical. Do not get to the medical stage of the selection process and fail on something that could have been avoided through carrying out some form of prior fitness training. Within this guide I have provided you with a FREE 'How to get Paramedic Fit' information guide, which details the tests you will undertake, but more importantly how to prepare for them.

Start your exercise programme as soon as you apply to join and make sure the exercises you perform are relevant to the tests that you will undertake. One of the best exercises to prepare for the test is to perform 'step-ups', either at a gymnasium or on the bottom stair in your home. As they get easier and you become fitter, you can begin to incorporate the carrying of weights to increase the intensity of the exercises.

Don't just assume that you are fit enough – Make sure you are!

INSIDER TIP NUMBER 3 – LEARN WHAT THE JOB ENTAILS

As with any job that you apply for it is important to understand exactly what the job entails. Can you imagine attending the interview for becoming a paramedic and being asked the question – "Tell me about the role of a paramedic – what do they do?" and not being able to answer it! You can almost guarantee that you will be asked this question during your interview so you need to research the role fully. To begin with, read the 'person specification' of the role you are applying for. This will give you some excellent information about what the job entails and what is expected of you.

During the selection process, try to visit your local ambulance station and talk to the staff there about their role and what it involves. They will be able to give you an invaluable insight into their work, the good sides of the job and also the elements that test their skills and their resolve.

It is also important that you visit the website of the NHS trust you are applying to join – you will find some very useful information here to help you.

So, be prepared to answer the following questions that relate to the role of a paramedic:

Q. What does the role of a paramedic or emergency care assistant involve?

Q. What shifts do they work and what does a typical working day consist of?

Q. What are the positive aspects of the job and what areas will test you?

Q. What has attracted you to this role and why should we choose you over the other applicants?

Q. What skills are required to become a paramedic or emergency care assistant and do you have them?

Those applicants who are successful in their application are usually those who have gone out of their way to make more of a 'focused' effort. If you prepare fully and spend the time finding out about the role then this will shine through during your interview.

INSIDER TIP NUMBER 4 – LEARN ABOUT THE NHS TRUST YOU ARE APPLYING FOR

It is very important that you learn about the NHS Trust or the organisation that you are applying to join.

During my career I sat on many interview panels assessing potential applicants for jobs in the emergency services and it amazed me how many people knew little or nothing about the organisation. Many of them were applying for a number of different services all at one time, and whilst there is nothing wrong with this, they had ultimately lost the ability to focus their preparation fully on one specific job with one specific organisation.

If you were an employer, and you were interviewing ten candidates for one position, what would expect them to know? To begin with you would expect them to have a thorough knowledge of the role they were applying for and also an in depth knowledge of the organisation. Those canidadtes who have both of these are more likely to be committed to the role, and more importantly the organisation. Remember, if you are successful, the NHS trust will spend literally thousands on your development and training so they want to be sure that you are committed to them and their organisation.

The first area to research is the website of the NHS trust you are applying for. Visit the website and absorb the information that is contained within it. Look to research topics such as the Race Equality Scheme, annual reports, good news stories, latest news, public campaigns, how many employees there are, when was that particular trust formed, who is the chief executive (or equivalent), how many paramedics do they have at the moment, what was their performance like for last year and what are the main makes of vehicles they use etc?

Once you have gathered this information, you then need to read your recruitment literature, thoroughly. Finally, during your visit to your local ambulance station, ask the crews what it is like to work for this particular organisation. They will be able to give you first hand information about the positive aspects of the trust and what it expects of its employees.

INSIDER TIP NUMBER 5 – PREPARE FULLY FOR THE INTERVIEW

Just because you have progressed to the interview, doesn't mean to say that you are guaranteed to pass or be accepted. You still have a long way to go. Having said that, the fact that you have progressed this far is a tremendous achievement and it means that the Ambulance Service is seriously interested in recruiting you. The same rules apply when applying to university – makes sure you are fully prepared for the interview.

During the interview they will be assessing a number of key areas including:

- Your knowledge of the role you are applying for

- Your knowledge of the NHS trust or organisation you have applied to join

- Your skills and experiences that are relevant to the role

- Your motivations for joining

- Additional subject knowledge and expertise

Each of the above five areas can be broken down into many different areas and within this guide I will help you to prepare for each of them

It is important that you stand out from the rest of the candidates and a good way to do this is to be knowledgeable in a number of subjects relating to both the role and the trust that you are applying for.

Don't just go to the interview expecting to be asked questions about your strengths and weaknesses. During the interview you will need to provide examples of where you match the person specification for the job you are applying for. Within the interview section of this guide you will find useful tips and advice to help you prepare for your responses.

Look at the sample interview questions provided and then use the templates provided to create your own responses based on your knowledge and experience.

INSIDER TIP NUMBER 6 – BE AWARE OF THE EQUALITY SCHEME FOR THE TRUST YOU ARE APPLYING TO JOIN

In order for an NHS Trust to meet its strategic aims it must develop what is called an Equality Scheme. Sometimes, this will be called an Equality and Inclusion scheme.

In very basic terms the Equality Scheme sets out the organisation's commitment to valuing people's differences, no matter what their race, ethnic and cultural background, disability, gender, gender identity, sexuality, religion and

beliefs, or age. It is not just the Ambulance Service who must produce such a scheme, but all public bodies including the Fire Service and the Police Force.

Many trusts will choose to develop and implement an individual Race Equality scheme, a Disability Equality scheme, a Gender Equality scheme and also an Age Equality scheme, whereas other trusts will choose to develop a single all-encompassing Equality Scheme. Regardless of which type of scheme they choose to implement, each NHS Trust must learn, develop and implement policies and strategies that provide equal access to all in an inclusive, non-discriminatory and culturally appropriate way.

This may all seem heavy-going, especially as you are applying for a job as a frontline paramedic or emergency care assistant. However, the Equality Scheme forms part of the mission and aims for the Trust that you are applying to join and therefore you should have a knowledge of its contents and what it stands for. You do not need to know the 'ins and outs' of the scheme, but just be aware of its content, the fact that it exists and also believe in it. The more you know about the Ambulance Service you are applying to join, the better.

You can almost guarantee that the other candidates will not even be aware of its existence. So, when the interview panel asks you to tell them what you know about their trust, you can tell them about this important documentation and the legislation that drives it.

Before you complete your application form, and attend the interview, I strongly advise that you obtain a copy of the Equality Scheme for the trust or organisation you are applying to join. The Equality Scheme can normally be found via the trust's website. During your preparation for the interview, try to obtain the scheme and have a read of the content.

Remember, you do not need to read it back to front, just be aware of it and what it stands for.

INSIDER TIP NUMBER 7 – UNDERSTAND DIVERSITY AND COMMUNITY AWARENESS

Diversity and community awareness are very important subjects that you must make yourself aware of before you apply to join the Ambulance Service. Let me break each one down individually and briefly look into what they each mean:

Diversity
Diveristy can be defined as:

"The concept of diversity encompasses acceptance and respect. It means understanding that each individual is unique, and recognising our individual differences. These can be along the dimensions of race, ethnicity, gender, sexual orientation, socio-economic status, age, physical abilities, religious beliefs, political beliefs, or other ideologies. It is the exploration of these differences in a safe, positive, and nurturing environment. It is about understanding each other and moving beyond simple tolerance to embracing and celebrating the rich dimensions of diversity contained within each individual."

As we are all aware, society is a diverse place, therefore so is the workplace. As a paramedic or emergency care assistant you will be required to work in a diverse society and you will also be required to work within a diverse workforce. Some people do not feel comfortable working with people from different cultures or backgrounds, and if this applies to you then the job of a paramedic or emergency care assistant is possibly not for you.

 how2become

A diverse workforce brings many benefits to an organisation and helps it to serve its community in a far more effective manner. If our community is diverse in nature, then the public services that represent it should be too.

You must be able to work with people from all cultures, backgrounds, ages, genders and disabilities. Every person in the workplace and within society has a contribution to make. If we were all exactly the same then the world would be a very boring place! Understand diversity, embrace it and most importantly believe in it.

Community Awareness

During the interview stage there is a possibility that you will be asked a question relating to your awareness of the community. Questions such as – *"What can you tell me about your local community and the problems you may face as a paramedic?"* have been used before during the interview.

Unless you are aware of your local community, its make-up, and the problems that you may encounter as a paramedic, then you will not be able to provide a good response.

Take a minute to think about your community and your local area. What problems do you think the local ambulance crews encounter when carrying out their job? Are the roads heavily congested? Is there a busy night time scene, which could lead to excessive alcohol consumption? Is the community diverse in nature, which could lead to communication problems when treating casualties who speak a different language to you? By asking yourself these questions you are starting to be more aware of your local community and the difficulties you could face as a paramedic.

The Ambulance Service needs to be aware of its community so they can provide the highest level of service to everybody. By

understanding the needs of the community, the Ambulance Service is then able to work towards making the necessary changes to how they operate.

INSIDER TIP NUMBER 8 – TRY TO ARRANGE A 'RIDE OUT'

What's a ride out?

A 'ride out' is the opportunity to go out with an ambulance crew for the day to have a close look at what the job entails. This can sometimes be achieved by contacting the duty station officer at your local ambulance station and arranging the 'ride out' with an experienced crew.

If permitted, you will be required to complete a form that includes a disclaimer. You will then be required to arrange a short term temporary Personal Liability Insurance through your insurance broker. Before commencing the 'ride out' you will be required to produce a cover note.

A 'ride out' is an excellent method of finding out about the role that you are applying for and it will assist you with your answers during the interview. It will also demonstrate to the interview panel that you have truly gone out of your way to find out what the job entails. When the panel ask you the question – *"Tell us what steps you have taken to find out about the job?"* then you will be able to provide a first class response and go into fine detail about what the job entails.

If you are unable to arrange the 'ride out', at the very least arrange a visit to your local ambulance station to talk to the duty crew and have a look around the station. During your visit, ask as many questions as possible about the role, the equipment they use, the best and worst aspects of the job and the training.

Go out of your way to beat the competition!

INSIDER TIP NUMBER 9 –
IMPROVE YOUR MAP READING SKILLS

Imagine the scene – You are serving at a busy ambulance station that responds to an average of 26 calls per day. It is 4am on a cold and frosty winter's morning. You receive a 999 call to an elderly man who the caller believes is suffering from a heart attack. You need to get there fast. The driver of the ambulance is concentrating on the icy roads and it is your job to use a map to find the road, and also provide the driver with exact directions. If you make a mistake or take a wrong turn then it could make the difference between life and death. Could you do it?

If you cannot use or read a map then you need to learn how to before you go to your assessment. Not every NHS trust uses this form of testing during the selection test. However, there are a number who do. Map reading is an integral part of a paramedic's job and being able to read a map quickly and effectively is essential.

In order to practise, all you need to do is purchase a map of your local town or area. Start to use the map when you are out and about and get a feel for how the coordinates of the map work. The interview panel may ask you to talk them through how to read a map so make sure you are competent in this area.

INSIDER TIP NUMBER 10 – READ THE HIGHWAY CODE AND IMPROVE YOUR DRIVING SKILLS

During the selection process you will be required to undertake a driving assessment, which consists of a pre-driving check, a familiarisation drive, a test drive and an oral or written Highway Code Assessment. Don't leave it to chance that you will pass.

Purchase the Highway Code and read it. Get a friend, relative or partner to ask you questions about the Highway Code. Practise your reversing skills in a car park and make sure you perform manoeuvres in the correct manner.

Although this is not necessary, you may wish to pay for some familiarisation driving lessons to brush up on your skills and to ensure you are carrying out manoeuvres correctly.

BONUS TIP
INSIDER TIP NUMBER 11 – LEARN THE CRITICAL VALUES OF THE AMBULANCE SERVICE YOU ARE ATTEMPTING TO JOIN

Each ambulance service will have a number of values that it upholds. It will also expect its employees to uphold the values to. Therefore, there is a strong chance that you will be tested against these values either directly at interview or via an online assessment.

It is vitally important that you learn and understand these values and are able to recite them word for word before you attend the interview. You will be able to find the values on the website of the service you are applying to join.

Here are a few examples of the types of values an ambulance service will work to:

Providing clinical excellence
This means that the service will provide the highest standards of patient care. They will be considerate, kind, compassionate, caring and act in a manner that is appropriate to the patient's needs at all times.

Be professional
The service will aim to be highly professional in everything it does.

Be respectful and courteous

Each service must value diversity and treat everyone as they would wish to be treated. Any forms of bullying, discrimination or inappropriate actions will not be tolerated.

Integrity

The service will be open and honest in all that it does and act to set standards of behaviour and conduct.

Work effectively as a team

The service will listen to the views and opinions of its team. It will take a genuine interest in the development of its staff and provide encouragement when needed.

Communication

The service will communicate relevant messages to both its staff and the community that it serves.

Be responsible

The service will act in a responsible manner at all times and be accountable for its actions.

Leadership and direction

The service will lead by example and act with pride, passion and determination.

BONUS TIP
INSIDER TIP NUMBER 12 – CARRY OUT SOME FORM OF COMMUNITY OR CHARITY WORK

If I was applying to become a paramedic or emergency care assistant today, then part of my preparation would be to work in the community, or even carry out some form of charity work.

You will recall that I placed a large emphasis on your knowledge of the community earlier on, and by following this tip you will be providing evidence of exactly that. As you will already know, paramedics are caring people. They work very closely within their communities in order to make them a safer place to live. Without them we would not survive.

If you can demonstrate on your application form, and during the interview, that you are genuinely a caring person then this will work in your favour. If I was the interviewer and you informed me during the interview that you currently carry out some form of community or charity work then I would be very impressed!

Examples of community/charity work

- Working a few hours per week in a local charity shop.

- Helping out at your local community centre.

- Organising and carrying out a charity car wash at your local supermarket.

- Running a race for charity.

- Sponsored cycle or swim.

CHAPTER FIVE
THE APPLICATION FORM

The application form is the first stage of the selection process and also the stage where the majority of applicants fail. This stage of the selection process is just as important as the rest and it is crucial that you set aside plenty of time to complete it correctly. The application form that you submit may be used at the end of the selection process to further assess candidates, so give it the time and effort it deserves by following the advice and guidance that is contained within this section of your guide.

Most application forms can be accessed via the website of the Ambulance Service you are applying to join. If you do not have access to the internet then you can apply for a postal application pack by telephoning the service you wish to apply for. Some Ambulance Services are going over to an electronic version of the application form but the majority still used paper-based forms.

Before completing the application form you should consider the following points:

- Keep a regular check on the website of the trust you are applying to join for recruitment updates. As soon as they advertise vacancies then start working on your application form. Most candidates will submit their form right at the deadline. Whilst your form will usually be assessed at this late stage, some services operate a cut off point for the number of applications they receive so it is advisable to get your form submitted as soon as possible.

- Once you receive your application form, photocopy it at least twice. It is important that you complete a draft form first as this will allow you to iron out any mistakes.

- Before you start to complete the form, acquire and read the vision/mission statement and the patient charter of the service you are applying to join. This will give you a full understanding of what the service is trying to achieve. If you structure your responses around this vision/mission statement and the patient charter then your chances of success will increase.

- Be fully aware of the job description and, again, try to structure your responses to the questions around this.

- Complete the form in the correct colour ink (if completing a paper-based form) and by following the guidance notes to the letter. This may sound obvious but if you fail to follow simple instructions then your form will be rejected.

- Make sure your handwriting is neat and tidy and your grammar, punctuation and spelling are all correct – ask someone to proof read it before you submit it.

- Before you send off the completed form photocopy it and keep a copy for yourself. It is important that you refer back to the form prior to attending an interview.

- Consider posting your completed application form by recorded delivery. There have been many cases where forms have become lost in the post. If facilities to submit your application via electronic mail exist then make sure you obtain confirmation that it has been received.

MORE ABOUT THE APPLICATION FORM

You will normally be required to complete the application form in your own handwriting. However, many Ambulance Services now allow you to complete it online; CVs are not generally accepted.

Whilst application forms do vary, the majority of them consist of the following key areas:

Personal Details
This section of the form is relatively straightforward to complete and will consist of you name, your address and your contact details.

Right to work in the UK
This section is again simple to complete. The Ambulance Service will want to know that you have the right to work in the UK and you may be required to produce documentation to prove this at some stage during the selection process.

Equal Opportunities monitoring
This section allows the service to monitor and ensure that it is receiving applicants from all sections of the community. Again it is relatively simple to complete and is usually based on a 'tick box' format.

Criminal convictions

Before completing this section it is important to refer to the guidance notes that should be with your application pack.

Driving licence details and experience

Within this section you will normally be required to provide details of your driving licence, the categories you are qualified to drive, and also any relevant driving experience.

Education

This section requires you to submit details about your education and qualifications.

Job-related training

Some application forms will give you the opportunity to submit details about your experience and training that is relevant to the job you are applying for. If this is the case and you have relevant experience and training, then make sure you submit it. Examples of relevant training and courses would include:

- Health and safety training;

- Driver training;

- Fitness training and courses;

- Customer care training and courses;

- First aid training and courses;

- Manual handling training and courses.

Employment history and references

Every application form will request details of your employment history and references. It is important to check first with your nominated referees that they give their permission. Most

Ambulance Services will not request references until just prior to offering you the position.

If there are any gaps in your employment history then you will need to provide details of how you have spent your time. Those applicants who can demonstrate that they have used their time wisely will score higher marks. Examples of using time wisely in between employment include further education, training courses, voluntary or community work or looking after sick relatives.

Application form questions
At some point during the application form you will be asked to respond to at least one question that requires you to detail why you are applying for the post and also what you have to offer in terms of experience and personal skills.

Sickness and absence
Some Ambulance Services will require you to provide details of your sickness and absence on the form. It is important that you are honest when providing these details, as they will confirm them with you current or recent employer during the reference stage.

SAMPLE APPLICATION FORM QUESTION

'Why have you applied for this post and what experience and personal skills do you have to offer?'

If you fail to make an adequate response to this type of question you will not be short-listed, so take your time when preparing your response. As stated previously, you must ensure that you read the person specification for the role and give evidence where you have demonstrated these qualities in your work life or personal life.

You should provide details of your experience and training to demonstrate why you are suitable for this post. When describing your current or previous work, you should specify **your** responsibilities, rather than those of your department or team.

Address all the criteria on the person specification, showing how you meet these criteria. You should mention experience, skills, achievements and knowledge gained not only in past employment, but also through other activities such as voluntary or community work, experience in the home, and leisure interests. You should, where possible, give examples of specific situations that you have come across and how you have dealt with the situation and the people involved. You should also show how this experience relates to the position you are applying for.

Before you respond to this question read the guidance notes that are applicable to your particular form.

The following is a sample response to this type of question. Read the response carefully before using a blank sheet of paper to create your own based on your own skills, knowledge and experiences.

SAMPLE RESPONSE TO APPLICATION FORM QUESTION

'Why have you applied for this post and what experience and personal skills do you have to offer?'

"I believe I show self-discipline at work each day. I decide where, when, how and the duration I work for, and as part of a uniformed service I take pride in my personal appearance. I realise there will be times during my career when there will be great emotional strain placed on me.

I have applied for this post as I am confident that I have the necessary skills and attributes required to become a competent paramedic. Having studied the role in depth, and also the expectations of the service, I believe that the experience and knowledge that I have gained so far will be a valuable asset to the service. I have been particularly attracted to the role because it is predominantly focused on delivering a high standard of care to the community. I have been involved in a number of voluntary community roles in the past and I have found this to be extremely rewarding. I want to work in a role that is both varied, challenging and community focused.

In relation to my experiences and personal skills I have many that are applicable to the role and that I believe the service would benefit from. As a Royal Marines Commando I found myself in many stressful and unusual situations, experienced many cultures and travelled widely. The situations that I have experienced so far would allow me to adapt to the role of a paramedic quickly. I understand that the role includes a requirement to perform under pressure, the ability to work as part of a team and the importance of working to set procedures and policies. I have a large amount of experience in all of these areas. As I have become older I have developed

into a more rounded individual, I have utilised all the skills obtained during this time to further my career and personal life.

I now appreciate the importance of a stable home life and I am getting married in September. As a student paramedic I will be in the public eye. Self-discipline, professionalism and a mature outlook on life will be vital to ensure the continued good reputation that this Ambulance Service has with the general public."

FURTHER SAMPLE RESPONSES TO APPLICATION FORM QUESTIONS

Within this section I have provided you with a number of additional sample responses to possible application form questions. Read the questions first and then study the responses.

Don't forget to obtain a copy of both the 'person specification' and the vision statement of the service you are applying to join.

The responses that have been formulated on the following pages have been structured utilising the person specification and vision statements detailed earlier within this section.

Once you have read and understood the sample responses, use the template provided to construct your own. This is great practice for when you come to complete your own application form.

SAMPLE APPLICATION FORM QUESTION 1

Describe your skills, experience and achievements, particularly those that are directly related to the job you are applying for.

When answering this type of question try to formulate a response that relates to your skills and experience gained so far either in your personal life or work life. What have you done so far that relates to the person specification of the job you are applying for? Try to think of any work you have carried out that involves customer care skills and dealing with difficult people in a calm and sensitive manner. Are you a mature, dedicated, enthusiastic and disciplined person? If so then try to give examples where you have used these qualities.

SAMPLE RESPONSE TO APPLICATION FORM QUESTION 1

Describe your skills, experience and achievements, particularly those that are directly related to the job you are applying for.

"During my previous job as a customer services representative I was constantly presented with difficult and stressful situations, where a delicate skill of dealing with others was essential.

The experience I gained within this role has given me an understanding of what is required as a paramedic and emergency care assistant. The customer care skills I have acquired so far will give me a solid grounding to becoming a competent and reliable member of this Ambulance Service.

I currently act as a neighbourhood watch coordinator for my local Parish Council and take a great pride in my work, which

involves helping, supporting and caring for others. Within this voluntary role, I often find myself working alone and having to make difficult decisions that affect others. I fully understand that the Ambulance Service prides itself on its reputation to serve others who are in need and requires its staff to be disciplined, motivated and reliable.

I am dedicated, enthusiastic and committed to the values and vision of the Ambulance Service and believe that I would be a great asset to the team."

Now use the template on the following page to create your own response. Remember to use keywords and phrases from the vision, values of the NHS trust and also person specification of the role you are applying for. This will be excellent practise for when you come to complete the real thing.

TEMPLATE FOR SAMPLE APPLICATION FORM QUESTION 1

Describe your skills, experience and achievements, particularly those that are directly related to the job you are applying for.

SAMPLE APPLICATION FORM QUESTION 2

Please indicate why you are suitable for the position for which you have applied. You may wish to mention previous relevant experience, which may have been gained inside or outside a work situation.

Once again, look at the question being asked. It is asking you to demonstrate WHY you are suitable for the post. It also states that PREVIOUS EXPERIENCE is an option for inclusion within your response.

The following list gives examples of words, phrases and experience you may wish to consider including in your response:

- Motivated, dedicated, reliable, punctual;

- Committed to the aims and values of the service;

- Ability to deal with others in a sensitive and caring nature;

- Adaptable and flexible with an ability to accept organisational change;

- Any community or voluntary work that you have carried out;

- The skills you have already acquired in your current or previous role.

SAMPLE RESPONSE TO APPLICATION FORM QUESTION 2

Please indicate why you are suitable for the position for which you have applied. You may wish to mention previous relevant experience, which may have been gained inside or outside a work situation.

"I understand that working for the Ambulance Service will be difficult and stressful at times. The skills I have acquired so far in my current role as a traffic warden will assist me in this particular role. I am a disciplined person who has encountered many difficult situations whilst working with the general public. During any situation I have experienced so far I have always maintained a calm disposition, focusing on my role and the level of service we provide. On many occasions I have had to deal with people with tact, diplomacy and assertiveness and I believe my maturity and experience would be of great benefit to the Ambulance Service.

I go out of my way to learn new skills and I would be committed to both the role and vision of the service that I would be representing. I am reliable, committed, dedicated and enthusiastic and would make a good role model for the Ambulance Service in upholding its values and reputation."

Now use the following template to create your own individual response.

TEMPLATE FOR SAMPLE APPLICATION FORM QUESTION 2

Please indicate why you are suitable for the position for which you have applied. You may wish to mention previous relevant experience, which may have been gained inside or outside a work situation.

FINAL TIPS FOR COMPLETING A SUCCESSFUL APPLICATION FORM

- Before you complete the application form read the guidance notes carefully. Most applicants will not bother to read the guidance notes and they will lose precious marks as a result. For example, the guidance notes may tell you to complete **every** section. If you fail to follow a simple instruction like this then your form may be rejected. If any of the sections do not apply to you then you still need to write N/A or not applicable.

- Make sure you complete a draft copy of the application form first. You will definitely make mistakes the first time around.

- The person specification will usually include both 'essential' criteria and 'desirable' criteria. Only those candidates who provide details of how they meet every 'essential' criterion will progress through to the next stage. Do not assume that the person assessing your paper will know that you meet every 'essential' criterion. You must provide details of how you meet each and every one, this is very important!

- Some application forms will allow you to attach additional sheets of paper when responding to some of the questions on the form. If you decide to take up this option make sure you attach the sheets to the form. It is also important that you put your name at the top of each additional sheet just in case they become detached.

- Check to see whether the form asks you for copies of your educational qualifications. If it does, be sure to attach them. You will normally be required to provide the originals at interview.

- Don't forget to keep a copy of your completed application form for the interview stage and remember to send off your form by recorded delivery. If you are sending it by electronic mail, request confirmation that it has been received.

CHAPTER SIX

SAMPLE WRITTEN TESTS

During the selection process you may be required to undertake a number of psychometric tests. Whilst the type of tests will vary from trust to trust, the types of test that have been used in the past include:

- Verbal reasoning;

- Numerical reasoning;

- Map reading exercises;

- Dictation exercises.

In addition to the above tests and assessments you will also be required to take an oral Highway Code test.

Within this section I have provided you with a large number of tips and practice test questions covering each area. It is important to note that the following tests are provided as a practice aid only and they should not be relied upon to be an accurate reflection of the real tests.

HOW TO PREPARE FOR THE WRITTEN TESTS

It is crucial that you set aside plenty of time to prepare for the tests. Only you will know what areas you are competent in, and what areas you need to improve on. Whilst preparing for the tests you should aim for speed and accuracy. The more sample test questions you try, the faster and more accurate you will become. It is far better to practise a small number of tests every night in the build up to the tests rather than 'cramming' the night before. As soon as you have submitted your application form you should start preparing for the tests and interview.

Most applicants will wait until they hear whether or not their application form has been successful before sitting down and preparing for the tests, but this is losing them valuable preparation time. You need to start your preparation immediately! The results of the tests are used as part of the entire selection process and not in isolation. Just because a candidate achieves a lower than average score on the numerical tests, this does not automatically mean they can't become a highly competent paramedic. However a very poor score might be a cause for concern for the recruiter. You should be aiming for high scores in every element of the selection process, and that also includes the written tests.

Prior to the tests

- Preparation, preparation, preparation! In the weeks before the test, work hard to improve your skills in the testing areas. In addition to the tests contained within this guide there are numerous other testing resources available at www.how2become.com. Practise as many test questions as possible and make sure you learn from your mistakes!

- Get a good night's sleep before the test day and don't drink any alcohol or caffeine.

- On the morning of the test get up early and have a last practise at a small number of sample test questions just to get your brain working.

- Eat a good healthy breakfast such as bran flakes and a chopped up banana. Don't eat anything too heavy that will make you feel bloated or sluggish – remember; you want to be at your best! Drink plenty of water too.

- Check the news for any potential traffic problems and leave in good time to arrive at the test centre with plenty of time to spare. Take a small bottle of water with you to help keep you hydrated.

On The Day

- Arrive in good time at the test location. Make sure you know where the test centre is.

- Ensure that you know exactly what you are required to do – do not be afraid to ask questions.

- Follow the instructions you are given exactly.

- During the tests try to eliminate as many wrong answers as possible. For example, with numerical tests and verbal reasoning tests, a quick estimate may help you to discard several of the options without working out every alternative.

- Work as quickly and accurately as you can. Both speed and accuracy are important so do not spend too long on any one question.

- Do not waste time on a difficult question. If you are

stuck, leave it and move on but make sure you leave a space on the answer sheet.

• Don't worry if you do not finish all the questions in the time, but if you do, go over your answers again to check them.

• Wear smart, formal dress. Remember that you are trying to create a good impression. You are attempting to join a uniformed service so it is advisable that you wear an appropriate outfit. Many people at the test centre will be wearing jeans and trainers. Make sure you stand out for all the right reasons.

• Keep your head down and concentrate on the task in hand. It is your job to do as best as you possibly can during the tests so it is important that you concentrate.

Now work through each of the following sample testing exercises. Remember to work quickly and accurately.

Sample Verbal reasoning exercises

As part of the selection process you may be required to sit a verbal reasoning test. Part of the role of a paramedic requires you to understand, analyse and interpret written information that is of a complex or specialised nature.

Within this section I have provided you with three sample verbal reasoning tests to assist you during your preparation.

Exercise 1 consists of 30 multiple choice sample test questions. You have 9 minutes in which to complete the exercise.

The answers are provided at the end of the exercise.

VERBAL REASONING EXERCISE 1

1. Which of the following words is the odd one out?

A. Car   **B.** Aeroplane   **C.** Train   **D.** Bicycle   **E.** House

Answer [   ]

2. Which of the following is the odd one out?

A. Right   **B.** White   **C.** Dart   **D.** Bright   **E.** Sight

Answer [   ]

3. The following sentence has one word missing. Which
    ONE word makes the best sense of the sentence?

*The mechanic worked on the car for three hours. At the end
of the three hours he was . . . .*

A. Home   **B.** Rich   **C.** Crying   **D.** Exhausted   **E.** Thinking

Answer [   ]

4. The following sentence has 2 words missing. Which
    TWO words make best sense of the sentence?

*The man . . . . to walk along the beach with his dog.
He threw the stick and the dog . . . . it.*

A. Hated/Chose   **B.** Decided/Wanted

C. Liked/Chased   **D.** Hurried/Chased   **E.** Hated/Loved

Answer [   ]

5. In the line below, the word outside of the brackets will only go with four of the words inside the brackets to make longer words. Which ONE word will it not go with?

A	**B**	**C**	**D**

In (direct   famous   describable   cart)

Answer [   ]

6. In the line below, the word outside of the brackets will only go with four of the words inside the brackets to make longer words. Which ONE word will it NOT go with?

A	**B**	**C**	**D**

In (decisive   reference   destructible   convenience)

Answer [   ]

7. In the line below, the word outside of the brackets will only go with four of the words inside the brackets to make longer words. Which ONE word will it NOT go with?

A	**B**	**C**	**D**

A (float   bout   part   peck)

Answer [   ]

8.   Which of the following words is the odd one out?

A. Pink   **B.** Green   **C.** Ball   **D.** Red   **E.** Grey

Answer [   ]

9.   Which of the following words is the odd one out?

A. Run   **B.** Jog   **C.** Walk   **D.** Sit   **E.** Sprint

Answer [   ]

10. Which of the following words is the odd one out?

A. Eagle **B.** Plane **C.** Squirrel **D.** Cloud **E.** Bird

Answer [   ]

11. Which of the following words is the odd one out?

A. Gold   **B.** Ivory   **C.** Platinum   **D.** Bronze   **E.** Silver

Answer [   ]

12. Which of the following is the odd one out?

A. Pond   **B.** River   **C.** Stream   **D.** Brook   **E.** Ocean

Answer [   ]

13. Which of the following is the odd one out?

A. Wood   **B.** Chair   **C.** Table   **D.** Cupboard   **E.** Stool

Answer [   ]

14. Which three-letter word can be placed in front of the following words to make a new word?

Time   Break   Light   Dreamer

Answer [   ]

15. Which four-letter word can be placed in front of the following words to make a new word?

Box   Bag   Age   Card

Answer [   ]

16. The following sentence has one word missing. Which ONE word makes the best sense of the sentence?

After walking for an hour in search of the pub, David decided it was time to turn . . . . and go back home.

A. Up   **B.** In   **C.** Home   **D.** Around   **E.** Through

Answer [   ]

17. The following sentence has one word missing. Which ONE word makes the best sense of the sentence?

We are continually updating the site and would be . . . . to hear any comments you may have.

A. Pleased   **B.** Worried   **C.** Available   **D.** Suited   **E.** Scared

Answer

18. The following sentence has two words missing. Which TWO words make the best sense of the sentence?

The Fleet Air Arm is the Royal Navy's air force. It numbers some 6200 people, ... is 11.5% of the . . . . Royal Naval strength.

A. which/total   **B.** and/total   **C.** which/predicted

D. and/corporate   **E.** which/approximately

Answer

19. The following sentence has one word missing. Which ONE word makes the best sense of the sentence?

The Navy has had to . . . . and progress to be ever prepared to defend the British waters from rival forces.

A. Develop   **B.** Manoeuvre   **C.** Change   **D.** Seek   **E.** Watch

Answer

20. Which of the following is the odd one out?

A. Cat   **B.** Dog   **C.** Hamster   **D.** Owl   **E.** Rabbit

Answer [ ]

21. Which word best fits the following sentence?

My doctor says I smoke. It's bad for my health.

A. Cannot   **B.** Wouldn't   **C.** Shouldn't   **D.** Like   **E.** Might

Answer [ ]

22. Which word best fits the following exercise?

The best thing for a hangover is to go to bed and sleep it .

A. Through   **B.** Over   **C.** Away   **D.** In   **E.** Off

Answer [ ]

23. Complete the following sentence:

When Jane arrived at the disco, Andrew . . . .

A. Hadn't gone   **B.** Already left   **C.** Has already Left

D. Had not left   **E.** Had already left

Answer [ ]

24. Which of the following words is the odd one out?

A. Lawnmower **B.** Hose **C.** Rake **D.** Carpet **E.** Shovel

Answer [ ]

25. Complete the following sentence:

Karla was offered the job . . . . having poor qualifications.

A. Although **B.** Even though **C.** With

D. Without **E.** Despite

Answer [ ]

26. Complete the following sentence:

Not only . . . . to Glasgow, but he also visited many other places in Scotland too.

A. Did she **B.** Did he **C.** Did he go

D. She went **E.** She saw

Answer [ ]

27. Complete the following sentence:

Now please remember, you . . . . the test until the teacher tells you to.

A. Shouldn't **B.** Cannot be starting **C.** Are not to

D. Can't **E.** Are not to start

Answer [ ]

28. Which of the following is the odd one out?

A. Strawberry   **B.** Raspberry   **C.** Peach

D. Blackberry   **E.** Blueberry

Answer [   ]

29. Which of the following is the odd one out?

A. Football   **B.** Wrestling   **C.** Table tennis   **D.** Golf   **E.** Rugby

Answer [   ]

30. Which of the following is the odd one out?

A. Man   **B.** Milkman   **C.** Secretary

D. Policeman   **E.** Firefighter

Answer [   ]

ANSWERS TO VERBAL REASONING EXERCISE 1

1. E	16. D
2. C	17. A
3. D	18. A
4. C	19. A
5. D	20. D
6. B	21. C
7. D	22. E
8. C	23. E
9. D	24. D
10. C	25. E
11. B	26. C
12. A	27. E
13. A	28. C
14. Day	29. B
15. Post	30. A

VERBAL REASONING EXERCISE 2

Now that you have completed exercise 1, take a look at exercise 2, which is of a different nature.

Take a look at the following example question:

Choose the word that best completes the following sentence:

> *The men . . . . football until the sun went down.*

> **A.** kicked   **B.** played   **C.** lost   **D.** won   **E.** decided

The answer to the above questions is **B.**

Now take a look at the sample questions on the following pages.

Allow yourself 10 minutes to answer the 30 questions.

VERBAL REASONING EXERCISE 2

1.   Insert the missing word:

If you are . . . . at the written tests you will progress to the next stage.

A. Okay   **B.** Fail   **C.** Work   **D.** Successful   **E.** Pass

Answer [   ]

2.   Hot is to cold as wet is to?

A. Dry   **B.** Water   **C.** Slippery   **D.** Wash   **E.** Lake

Answer [   ]

3.   'Bona fide' means the same as?

A. Correct   **B.** Genuine   **C.** Guessing   **D.** Caring   **E.** Want

Answer [   ]

4.   Which of the following words is the closest to Horizontal?

A. Narrow   **B.** Vertical   **C.** Parallel   **D.** Round   **E.** Upwards

Answer [   ]

5. Insert the missing word:

After satisfactory . . . . of the medical, you will be measured for your uniform.

A. Pass **B.** Sample **C.** Attendance **D.** Completion **E.** Being

Answer

6. Listen is to hear as Talk is to?

A. Watch   **B.** Mouth   **C.** Write   **D.** Say   **E.** Speak

Answer

7. Which of the following words is closest to Gather?

A. Convene **B.** Around **C.** Stay **D.** Refute **E.** Disembark

Answer

8. Insert the missing word:

In order to . . . . the machinery you need to be qualified.

A. Direct **B.** Operate **C.** Qualify **D.** Change **E.** Assessed

Answer

9. Insert the missing word:

There are two aspects to . . . . good habits.

A. Organising   **B.** Unfolding   **C.** Making

D. Developing   **E.** Start

Answer

10. Skilful means the same as?

A. Creative   **B.** Adept   **C.** Efficient   **D.** Working   **E.** Watchful

Answer

11. Car is to drive as Aeroplane is to?

A. Holiday   **B.** Cabin Crew   **C.** Airport   **D.** Fly   **E.** Wing

Answer

12. Tall is to short as Big is to?

A. Small   **B.** Length   **C.** Line   **D.** Thinner   **E.** Metre

Answer

13. Train is to track as Ship is to?

A. Harbour   **B.** Sea   **C.** Sail   **D.** Stern   **E.** Hull

Answer

14. If the following words were arranged in alphabetical order, which one would be second?

A. Believe   **B.** Beast   **C.** Belief   **D.** Bereaved   **E.** Best

Answer [   ]

15. If the following words were arranged in alphabetical order, which one would be last?

A. Desire   **B.** Desired   **C.** Desirable

D. Deserted   **E.** Desert

Answer [   ]

16. Walk is to run as Slow is to?

A. Fast   **B.** Speed   **C.** Quicker   **D.** Pace   **E.** Stop

Answer [   ]

17. Sun is to hot as Ice is to?

A. Melt   **B.** Winter   **C.** Icicle   **D.** Freeze   **E.** Cold

Answer [   ]

18. Which of the following words is closest to the word Tentative?

A. Caring   **B.** Desire   **C.** Watching   **D.** Hesitant   **E.** Scared

Answer [   ]

19. Which of the following words is closest to Regulate?

A. Signal   **B.** Direct   **C.** Control   **D.** Change   **E.** Assess

Answer

20. Hair is to head as Shoe is to?

A. Foot   **B.** Slipper   **C.** Glove   **D.** Laces   **E.** Heel

Answer

21. Insert the missing word:

James . . . . the train and sat in First Class.

A. Climbed   **B.** Missed   **C.** Ran   **D.** Followed   **E.** Boarded

Answer

22. Which of the following words is closest to the meaning
of Desire?

A. Achieve   **B.** Wish   **C.** Get   **D.** Ascertain   **E.** Believe

Answer

23. Hammer is to nail as Bat is to?

A. Fly   **B.** Ball   **C.** Cricket   **D.** Cat   **E.** Hit

Answer

24. Book is to read as Music is to?

A. Note   **B.** Instrument   **C.** Listen   **D.** Dance   **E.** Piano

Answer [   ]

25. Which of the following words contains the most vowels?

A. Reasonable   **B.** Combination

C. Vegetables   **D.** Audaciously

Answer [   ]

26. Which of the following words contains the least vowels?

A. Barber   **B.** Radio   **C.** Disastrous   **D.** Elephant   **E.** March

Answer [   ]

27. Chair is to sit as Ladder is to?

A. Climb   **B.** Step   **C.** Bridge   **D.** Metal   **E.** Heavy

Answer [   ]

28. Mark can run faster than Jane. Jane can run faster than Nigel who is slower than Bill. Bill runs faster than Mark. Who is the slowest?

A. Nigel   **B.** Jane   **C.** Bill   **D.** Mark

Answer

29. If the following words were placed in alphabetical order, which one would be third?

A. Delightful   **B.** Delicious   **C.** Delayed

D. Delicate   **E.** Derail

Answer

30. Insert the missing word:

Provisional offers of employment are made subject to . . . . of references.

A. Receipt   **B.** Obtain

C. Gathering   **D.** Maintenance   **E.** The

Answer

ANSWERS TO VERBAL REASONING EXERCISE 2

1. D	16. C
2. A	17. E
3. B	18. D
4. C	19. C
5. D	20. A
6. E	21. E
7. A	22. B
8. B	23. B
9. D	24. C
10. B	25. D
11. D	26. E
12. A	27. A
13. B	28. A
14. C	29. B
15. B	30. A

VERBAL REASONING COMPREHENSION EXERCISE

Another form of verbal reasoning assessment is the comprehension exercise.

This test usually includes a number of short passages of text followed by statements based on the information given in the passage. You are required to indicate whether the statements are true, false or cannot say, based on the information provided. When responding to these questions, use only the information provided in the passage and do not try to answer them in the light of any more detailed knowledge that you personally may have.

Take a look at the following sample question:

Sample question
Read the following passage before answering the question as true, false or cannot say.

Self discipline is a crucial element to the role of a paramedic. Without self discipline the paramedic will not perform his or her role competently. In relation to 'self discipline' the paramedic must be committed to keeping up to date with policies, procedures and also their own continuous professional development. In addition to these important areas they must also be committed to upholding the values of the ambulance Service and maintain a high standard of work at all times.

Question 1
In order to maintain self discipline the paramedic must be committed to keeping up to date with policies.

Answer | True | Based on the information provided the answer is true.

Now try the following sample questions. Remember to base your answers solely on the information provided in each passage. There are ten exercises in total and you have twenty minutes in which to complete them.

VERBAL REASONING COMPREHENSION EXERCISE 1

Read the following passage before answering the question as true, false or cannot say.

Paramedics are the senior ambulance service healthcare professionals at an emergency incident or accident. They are required to work on their own or as part of a highly trained team, which can include other health professionals such as emergency care assistants.

When they arrive at the scene of the incident their job is to assess the condition of the patient and provide the appropriate level of treatment and care. The equipment they use to assess a patient's condition is highly technical.

Question 1
Paramedics always work on their own at emergency incidents or accidents.

Question 2
Paramedics wear high visibility clothing at road traffic collisions to ensure they are safe.

Question 3
Upon arrival at the scene, the paramedic will assess the patient and provide the appropriate level of care.

VERBAL REASONING COMPREHENSION EXERCISE 2

Read the following passage before answering the question as true, false or cannot say.

Each ambulance service has a vision, which is designed to meet the needs of the public, the community and the patients that it cares for. It is the responsibility of each member of staff who works for the service to uphold the principles of the vision by ensuring they are well trained, caring, enthusiastic and proud of the job they do.

In addition to the vision, there will be a number of important values that act as a reminder to each employee of his or her responsibilities. Examples of these values include having the commitment to deliver the highest standard of patient care, being respectful to everyone both at work and within the community, acting with a high degree of integrity, and working together as an effective team. Finally, each individual will be responsible for his/her own actions.

Question 1
It is the responsibility of each member of staff to uphold the principles of the vision.

Question 2
In order to remind each employee of their responsibilities, there are a number of values.

Question 3
Examples of these values include communication and leadership and direction.

VERBAL REASONING COMPREHENSION EXERCISE 3

Read the following passage before answering the question as true, false or cannot say.

In order to ensure safe, secure and healthy communities, each county council will work closely together with partnership organisations such as the ambulance service, the police force, the fire service and the probation service under what is called a 'Community Safety Partnership'.

It is the responsibility of each Community Safety Partnership to look for ways to make the community a safer place to live through effective strategies and activities. Examples of problems that the Community Safety Partnership aims to tackle include alcohol-related crime, accidents and drugs.

During the Community Safety Partnership meetings, the Ambulance Service are able to provide accurate information about the problems they are facing during operational incidents.

Question 1
The Community Safety Partnership does not aim to tackle the problems of alcohol-related crime, accidents and drugs.

Question 2
The ambulance service will provide the Community Safety Partnership with accurate information about the problems they are facing during operational incidents.

Question 3
Within the community, burglary and theft from motor vehicles is a big problem.

VERBAL REASONING COMPREHENSION EXERCISE 4

Read the following passage before answering the question as true, false or cannot say.

The patient transport service (PTS) is a branch of the ambulance service that many people are unaware of. The role of the patient transport service includes transferring non-urgent patients to different hospitals, transporting geriatric and psycho geriatric patients and also routine discharges and admissions.

The PTS ambulances are usually driven by ambulance care assistants. They are trained in a wide variety of techniques including comprehensive first aid skills, specialist driving, manual handling and patient care. In order for the patient transport service to effectively carry their patients, they use specially designed vehicles with tail lifts.

Within some ambulance services a number of patient transport services crews are specially trained as a high dependency team. These are available for patients with specific clinical needs during transport. Although the work of PTS crews does not involve emergency duties it is crucial to the efficient running of the ambulance service.

Question 1
The patient transport service is a totally separate unit and does not form part of the ambulance service.

Question 2
The work that PTS crews undertake involves attending emergency incidents.

Question 3
The PTS ambulances are usually driven by emergency care assistants.

VERBAL REASONING COMPREHENSION EXERCISE 5

Read the following passage before answering the question as true, false or cannot say.

No two heart attacks are the same. Symptoms can range from feeling generally unwell to severe chest pain. In many cases chest pain or tightness is accompanied by a range of other symptoms.

The most common symptoms of heart attack are:

- Central chest pain that can spread to the arms, neck or jaw.

- Feeling sick or sweaty as well as having central chest pain.

- Feeling short of breath as well as having central chest pain.

Symptoms vary and some people may feel any of the following:

- A dull pain, ache, or 'heavy' feeling in the chest.

- A mild discomfort in the chest that makes you feel generally unwell.

- A pain in the chest that can spread to the back or stomach.

- A chest pain that feels like bad indigestion.

- Feeling light-headed or dizzy as well as having chest pain.

The pain can last from five minutes to several hours. Moving around, changing your position or resting will not stop or ease the pain. The pain may be constant or it may come and go. It may feel like pressure, squeezing or 'fullness'.

If you think that you, or someone you know is suffering from a heart attack you need to call 999 for an ambulance immediately.

Question 1
Heart attacks are always the same, including the symptoms.

Question 2
One of the symptoms of a heart attack includes a mild comfort in the chest that makes you feel well.

Question 3
When calling 999 you need to provide exact details of the patient's condition and their location.

VERBAL REASONING COMPREHENSION EXERCISE 6

Read the following passage before answering the question as true, false or cannot say.

When a member of the public dials 999 and requests the ambulance service, they can assist the call operator by having a number of important facts about the incident with them. These important facts include the following:

- The address of the incident, including the postcode.
- The phone number you are calling from.
- Details of the incident or accident that has occurred.

It is important that the caller provides this information so that the call operator can dispatch the relevant response as soon as possible to help.

In addition to the above information, you will also be asked to provide:

- The patient's age, sex and medical history;
- Whether the patient is conscious, breathing and if there is any bleeding or chest pain; and
- Details of the injury and how it happened.

Answering these questions will allow the call operator to pass on vital information to the ambulance crews who are on their way. As soon as they arrive they can start to provide the appropriate level of care. You should only call 999 in a genuine emergency.

Question 1
Providing the important facts about the incident to the call operator allows them to dispatch the relevant response as soon as possible.

Question 2

A caller may be asked to provide details of the patient's age, sex and medical history.

Question 3

You cannot call 999 during a genuine emergency.

VERBAL REASONING COMPREHENSION EXERCISE 7

Read the following passage before answering the question as true, false or cannot say.

Alcohol-related calls currently make up approximately six per cent of the workload of the ambulance service. In some instances an ambulance service will attend over 50,000 such incidents every year. This can put unnecessary pressure on the service due to some people who refuse to enjoy drink responsibly.

Some people become ill through drinking too much but there are also a large number of people who become injured as a result of being under the influence of alcohol. An unfortunate fact is that whilst the ambulance is attending to these avoidable incidents, they are not free to attend those patients who really need their help. There have also been a number of cases where ambulance crews have been attacked by those people they are trying to help.

It is the responsibility of each individual to drink safely and to think about how much they are drinking.

Question 1
Alcohol-related calls are a huge problem for the ambulance service.

Question 2
Ambulances have been attacked by some people who are under the influence of alcohol.

Question 3
It is the responsibility of each individual to drink safely and to think about how much they are drinking.

VERBAL REASONING COMPREHENSION EXERCISE 8

Read the following passage before answering the question as true, false or cannot say.

The role of a paramedic is highly challenging. Not only are paramedics required to care for patients who are either ill, injured or suffering from physical or mental conditions, they must also learn and absorb a large amount of job-relevant technical information. For a paramedic, no two days are the same. Typical work activities include responding to 999 calls, assessing the condition of casualties and providing the appropriate level of care, applying splints and administering pain relief, using various items of equipment including ventilators to assist breathing, carrying out surgical procedures, cleaning and decontaminating vehicles and equipment and writing up case notes relevant to each patient's history, condition and treatment.

In order to become a paramedic and work in the NHS you must be registered with the Health Professionals Council (HPC). Some training courses have been approved by the HPC and these can lead to a diploma, foundation degree and/or BSc honours degree in paramedic science. Students will usually have the option to study over 2-5 years depending on the course. Some NHS trusts are also employing 'student paramedics'. Upon successful completion of this course, which usually lasts 3 years, the student will become fully qualified as a paramedic.

Question 1
For a paramedic, no two days are the same. Typical work activities include answering 999 calls.

Question 2
In order to become a qualified paramedic you must complete a course with the Health Professionals Council (HPC)

Question 3
Upon successful completion of the 'student paramedic' course the student will become fully qualified as a paramedic.

VERBAL REASONING COMPREHENSION EXERCISE 9

Read the following passage before answering the question as true, false or cannot say.

Manual handling is a major cause of injuries in UK. Paramedics are required to lift and carry heavy items of equipment and even patients on some occasions. Wherever possible the need to manually handle equipment and patients should be avoided by using some form of appropriate equipment. However, if manual handling is unavoidable then the paramedic must assess and minimise the risks. If they are required to carry out manual handling techniques then these should always be done in line with their training, guidance and procedures.

Before lifting heavy items of equipment it is advisable that you:

1. Think before lifting and handling – You should plan the lift first. Can you use handling aids? Where are you taking the load and will you need assistance? Which route will you take?

2. Keep the load close to the waist – The load should be kept close to the body, with the heaviest side nearest. If a close approach to the load is not possible, try to slide it towards the body before attempting to lift it.

3. Ensure your position is stable – By keeping your feet apart with one leg slightly forward you will be able to maintain balance). Your feet should be moved to maintain balance during the lift. Avoid tight clothing and unsuitable footwear, which might impair movement.

4. Hold the load securely – If possible you should hug the load close to your body.

5. Keep and maintain good posture – At the start of the lift, slight bending of the back, hips and knees is preferable to fully flexing the back (stooping) or fully flexing the hips or knees (squatting).

6. Avoid any unnecessary flexing or twisting of the back whilst lifting. You should also avoid leaning sideways. All of these can lead to injury. Your shoulders should be level and facing in the same direction as your hips. Turning by moving the feet is better than twisting and lifting at the same time.

7. Keep your head up – Make sure you look ahead once the load is held securely.

8. Put the load down first before adjusting.

Question 1
At the start of the lift, stooping and squatting is preferable a slight bending of the back, hips and knees.

Question 2
Paramedics must carry out manual handling techniques in line with their training, guidance and procedures.

Question 3
Before lifting and handling you should plan the lift first. Part of this process includes wearing the right form of personal protective equipment (PPE).

VERBAL REASONING COMPREHENSION EXERCISE 10

Read the following passage before answering the question as true, false or cannot say.

Those applicants who are preparing to pass the paramedic selection process must ensure that they are fully prepared and focused. Part of their preparation includes the need to study the role of a paramedic in detail. They can achieve this by arranging a visit to their local ambulance station and discussing the role with current serving paramedics. They should also study their recruitment literature in detail, visit the website of the ambulance service they are applying to join and also read the vision and values of the trust.

The vision and values are an integral part of the trust's commitment to delivering an excellent service to the community it serves. Part of the vision includes a requirement of all staff to be well trained, caring, enthusiastic and proud of the job they do. Every member of staff who works for the ambulance service must also value diversity. This means that they should treat everyone with dignity and respect and this applies to not just their work colleagues, but members of the community too.

Another important element that forms part of the values of the ambulance service is that of clinical excellence. This means a commitment to providing the highest level of patient care and being kind, caring, ethical, considerate and responding appropriately to the needs of each patient.

Question 1
Valuing diversity means treating everyone with dignity and respect.

Question 2

Applicants who are preparing to pass the paramedic selection process can increase their chances of success by studying their recruitment literature in detail, visiting the website of the ambulance service they are applying to join and by also reading the vision and values of the trust.

Question 3

Part of the values of the ambulance service includes a requirement of each employee to work effectively as a team.

ANSWERS TO VERBAL REASONING COMPREHENSION EXERCISES

Exercise 1

1. False

2. Cannot say

3. True

Exercise 2

1. True

2. True

3. Cannot say

Exercise 3

1. False

2. True

3. Cannot say

Exercise 4

1. False

2. False

3. False

Exercise 5

1. False

2. False

3. Cannot say

Exercise 6

1. True

2. False

3. False

Exercise 7

1. Cannot say

2. Cannot say

3. True

Exercise 8

1. False

2. False

3. True

Exercise 9

1. False

2. True

3. Cannot say

Exercise 10

1. True

2. True

3. Cannot say

NUMERICAL REASONING EXERCISES

During the selection process to become a paramedic you may also have to sit a numerical reasoning test. On the following pages we have supplied you with a number of sample numerical reasoning test questions that are designed to assess your ability to interpret data using graphs and tables.

You must ensure that you read each question carefully so that you understand exactly what is required.

Now take a look at the exercise on the following page, which consists of 25 questions. You have 25 minutes in which to complete the exercise without the use of a calculator.

NUMERICAL REASONING EXERCISE 1

1. What is the missing number?

1   4   16   ?   256

Answer [   ]

2. What is the missing number?

$50/5 = 12 - ?$

Answer [   ]

3. What is the missing number?

$86 - 9 = 56 + ?$

Answer [   ]

4. What is the missing number?

$48/8 = ? - 8$

Answer [   ]

5. What is the missing number?

$30/0.6 = ?$

Answer [   ]

how2become

6. Which is the largest fraction?

3/4 7/8 4/5 7/9 1/4

Answer [   ]

7. If bananas cost 95p for 7 how many can you buy for £3.50?

A. 18   **B.** 19   **C.** 20   **D.** 21   **E.** 22

Answer [   ]

8. A car left Manchester at 06.43am and arrived in Kent, 239 miles away, at 10.58am. What was its average speed in miles per hour?

Answer [   ]

9. A jumbo jet flies 830 miles in 60 minutes. How many miles does it fly in 3 hours 30 minutes assuming a constant speed?

Answer [   ]

10. You get a wage increase of 7% plus an extra £8 per week. Your current wages are £245 per week. How much will your new wage be per week?

Answer [   ]

11. A cube has a volume of 27 cubic metres. If each side is doubled in length, what will its new volume be in cubic metres?

Answer

12. A driver drives 7 km North, then 4 km East, and then 1 km South. She then drives 5 km West before driving 1 km South and finally 1 km East. How many kilometres is she from her starting point?

Answer

13. A train travelling at 60 mph enters a tunnel that is 3 miles long. The train is one mile long. How many minutes does it take for the whole train to pass through the tunnel?

Answer

14. Steve and Sue both drive to their new home, which is 300 miles away. Steve drives the family car at an average speed of 50 mph. Sue drives their van at an average speed of 30 mph. During the journey, Steve stops for a total of 1 hour and 30 minutes; Sue stops for half as long. What is the difference in minutes between their arrival times?

Answer

15. It costs a manufacturing company £1.50 per component to make the first 1,000 components. All subsequent components then cost 75p each. How much will it cost to manufacture 4,000 components?

Answer [   ]

16. What's the missing number?

3   15   26   ?   45   53

Answer [   ]

17. Which of the following is the odd one out?

5   9   10   35   20   75

Answer [   ]

18. If $a + 2a + 3a = 6b - 12$ and if $b = 2$, what is the value of a?

Answer [   ]

19. $(11 \times 2 \times 2) + (8 \times 2) - 6 = ?$

Answer [   ]

20. $(27 \div 3 + 9) \times 2 - 7 = ?$

Answer [   ]

21. $72 \div 9 + 16 - ? = 20$

Answer

22. 40% of 125 = 250 ÷ ?

Answer

23. 80 % of 150 = ? × 12

Answer

24. If a football club sells the following amount of season tickets each year, what is the average number sold per year over the 4-year period?

Year 1 – 35,600 tickets sold

Year 2 – 35,400 tickets sold

Year 3 – 34,500 tickets sold

Year 4 – 33,500 tickets sold

Answer

25. $(450 \div 45 + 111) \div 11 = ?$

Answer

ANSWERS TO NUMERICAL REASONING EXERCISE 1

1. 64
2. 2
3. 21
4. 14
5. 50
6. 7/8
7. 21
8. 56.2 miles per hour
9. 2905 miles
10. £270.15
11. 216 m³
12. 5 km
13. 4 minutes

14. 205 minutes
15. £3750
16. 36
17. 9
18. 0
19. 54
20. 29
21. 4
22. 5
23. 1440
24. 34,750
25. 11

Now that you have completed the first numerical reasoning exercise, move on to the next set of exercises. There is no time limit with these exercises but try to work as quickly and accurately as possible.

Try to work without a calculator.

how2become

NUMERICAL REASONING EXERCISE 2

Study Table 1 before answering the following questions.

The following table lists the type of bonus each member of staff will receive if they reach a specific number of sales per hour they work. The table has not yet been completed. Staff work 7 hour shifts. To answer the questions you will need to complete the table.

Note: If a worker achieves 160 sales or more during their 7 hour shift they will receive an additional £50 bonus.

Time	10 sales	20 sales	30 sales	40 sales
1st hour	£21.00	£41.50	60.50	£72.00
2nd hour	£18.00	£35.00	£52.00	£60.00
3rd hour	£15.00	£28.50	£43.50	£50.00
4th hour		£22.00	£35.00	£42.00
5th hour	£9.00		£26.50	£36.00
6th hour	£6.00	£9.00		£32.00
7th hour	£3.00	£2.50	£9.50	

1. If the table was complete, how much could a worker earn in bonuses if they reached 10 sales every hour of their 7-hour shift?

A. £81   **B.** £84   **C.** £91   **D.** £85   **E.** £94

Answer [   ]

2. How much would a worker earn in bonuses if they reached 30 sales per hour for the first 3 hours of their shift and 40 sales per hour for the remaining 4 hours of their shift?

A. £292   **B.** £293   **C.** £436   **D.** £246   **E.** £296

Answer

3. How much would a worker earn in bonuses if they reached 10 sales during their first and last hour, 20 sales during the 2nd and 6th hours, 30 sales during the 3rd and 5th hours and 40 sales during the 4th hour?

A. £230   **B.** £250   **C.** £180   **D.** £181   **E.** £182

Answer

NUMERICAL REASONING EXERCISE 3

The following chart indicates the total number of cars manufactured per day of the week at the Arlingford Car Depot.

Study the graph and then answer the questions.

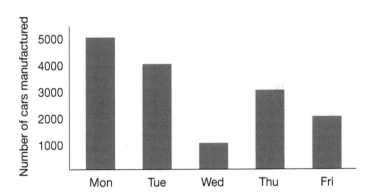

1. On which day was the number of cars manufactured 80% less than the number it was on Monday?

A. Tuesday   **B.** Wednesday   **C.** Thursday

D. Friday   **E.** None

Answer [   ]

2. How many cars were produced in total on Tuesday, Wednesday and Friday?

A. 4,000   **B.** 5,000   **C.** 6,000   **D.** 7,000   **E.** 8,000

Answer [   ]

3. What was the average number of cars manufactured per day for the working week?

A. 2142   **B.** 2500   **C.** 3000   **D.** 2141   **E.** 2140

Answer

NUMERICAL REASONING EXERCISE 4

The following graph indicates the total monthly profits for 4 competing companies. Study the graph before answering the questions.

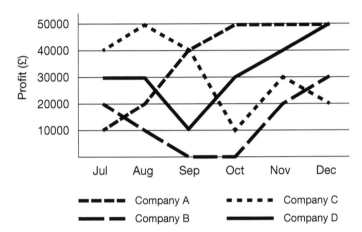

1. Over the 6-month period, which company made the greatest profit?

A. Company A   **B.** Company B

C. Company C   **D.** Company D

Answer [   ]

2. What was the difference in profits over the 6-month period between company C and company D?

A. £1,000   **B.** Nothing   **C.** £2,000   **D.** £3,000   **E.** £4,000

Answer [   ]

3. What was the total 6-month profit of all the four companies?

A. £660,000   **B.** £610,000   **C.** £630,000

D. £650,000   **E.** £690,000

Answer [   ]

NUMERICAL REASONING EXERCISE 5

Study Table 2 before answering the following questions.

The following table shows the distribution list for a UK based company including location of delivery, type of package ordered, the quantity ordered and the cost excluding delivery.

Date	Location of Delivery	Package ordered	Quantity ordered	Cost (excl. delivery)
13th Jan	Kent	Package 1	2	£45
17th Jan	Preston	Package 4	13	£1,600
2nd Feb	Manchester	Package 2	6	£246
3rd Feb	Glasgow		12	£270
17th Feb	Fareham	Package 2	8	
19th Mar	Huddersfield	Package 5	1	£213
20th Mar	Crewe		3	£639

1. Which package will be delivered on the 3rd of February?

A. Package 1   **B.** Package 2   **C.** Package 4   **D.** Package 5

Answer

2. What will be the cost (excluding delivery) on the 17th of February?

A. £322   **B.** £324   **C.** £326   **D.** £328   **E.** £330

Answer

3. Which package is scheduled to be delivered to Crewe on the 20th of March?

A. Package 1   **B.** Package 2   **C.** Package 4   **D.** Package 5

Answer [   ]

NUMERICAL REASONING EXERCISE 6

The following bar chart indicates the total number of people employed by a large international distribution company. Study the chart before answering the following questions.

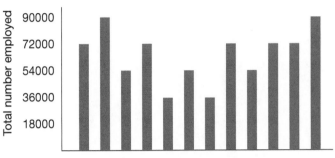

Jan Feb Mar Apr May Jun Jul Aug Sep Oct Nov Dec

1. What was the average monthly employment figure for the 12-month period?

A. 60000   **B.** 50000   **C.** 54500   **D.** 64500   **E.** 74500

Answer

2. What was the total number of people employed during the second quarter of the year?

A. 62000   **B.** 52000   **C.** 162000   **D.** 152000   **E.** 143000

Answer

3. What was the total difference in the number of people employed in the first quarter and the last quarter of the year?

A. 18000   **B.** 17000   **C.** 16000   **D.** 180000   **E.** 170000

Answer [   ]

ANSWERS TO NUMERICAL REASONING EXERCISES

Exercise 2

1. B

2. E

3. C

Exercise 3

1. B

2. D

3. C

Exercise 4

1. A

2. B

3. E

Exercise 5

1. A

2. D

3. D

Exercise 6

1. D

2. C

3. A

MAP-READING SKILLS

Some Ambulance Services will require you to take a map-reading test. However, with the introduction of satellite navigation systems this form of testing is on the decrease. I still advise that you learn how to use a map, just in case you need to for selection purposes, and also to answer any questions relating to this subject during the interview.

On the following pages I have provided you with explanations and sample exercises to help you prepare improve your map reading skills.

What is a map?
A map is basically a plan of the ground put on paper. Most maps, and the ones you will use during your service with the ambulance service, are drawn as the land would be seen from directly above.

Most maps have the following features:

- Motorways, public highways and footpaths.

- Landmarks, famous places and features.

- Contour lines to show the height above or below sea level.

- A key to show you what the symbols on the map actually mean. These are normally found at the beginning of the map and not on each page.

- A grid system of vertical and horizontal lines to help you pinpoint your exact location.

Understanding the map
Many public services such as the Police, Fire and Ambulance Service use maps as opposed to satellite navigation systems. Although the use of satellite navigation systems is becoming more and more common, they are still required to be capable

of using a map in case the navigation system becomes defective.

The maps are generally made up of a grid, which includes a series of lines that make up the grid (see diagram below).

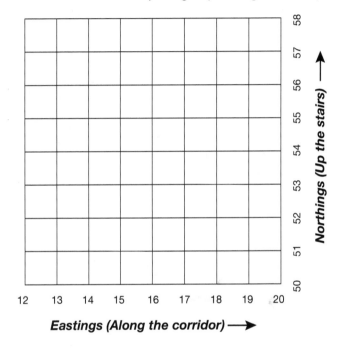

Eastings (Along the corridor) ⟶

To read the map we need to understand that the figures along the bottom, from left to right, are known as the EASTINGS and the figures that run up the side, from the bottom to the top, are called the NORTHINGS.

You will normally come across 2 different types of map reference:

1.   4-figure map reference
2.   6-figure map reference

An example of a 4-figure map reference would be 1365, which represents a kilometre square on an Ordnance Survey map.

An example of a 6-figure map reference would be 195640, which pinpoints an exact position on an Ordnance Survey map.

4-figure map references

When giving a 4-figure map reference you should always give the **EASTINGS** number first followed by the **NORTHINGS** number second.

Take a look at the grey square on the map below and you will notice that, using the above method, the grey block is located in square number 1554.

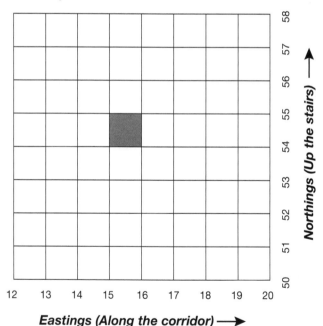

4-figure map references

Now take a look at the map below. Write down in the spaces provided the 4-figure map references of the indicated four grey boxes.

The answers are at the bottom of the page.

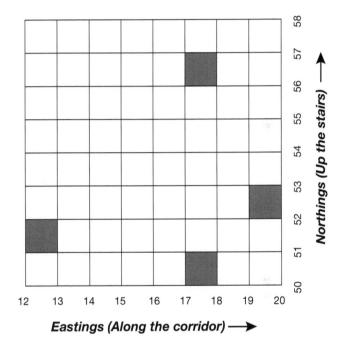

Eastings (Along the corridor) ➜

1st box		2nd box	

3rd box		4th box	

Answers: 1251; 1750; 1952; 1756

6-figure map references

When giving a 6-figure map reference, once again you should always give the **EASTINGS** number first followed by the **NORTHINGS** number second. Take a look at the grey square on the map below and you will notice that using the above method it is located in square **number** 191627.

However, on some maps, the lines and numbers that represent the 'tenths' will not be visible and you will have to divide the box into sections without the use of visible lines.

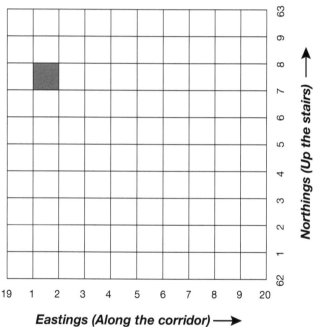

Eastings (Along the corridor) ⟶

6-figure map references

Now take a look at the map below. Write down in the spaces provided the 6-figure map reference of the two red squares, without the aid of the 'tenth' indication lines and numbers.

The answers are provided at the bottom of the page.

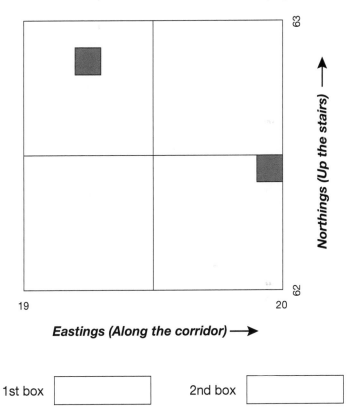

Eastings (Along the corridor) ➤

1st box [ ]   2nd box [ ]

Answers: 192628; 199624

MAP READING SKILLS EXERCISES

On the following pages I have provided you with four exercises to assist you in your preparation. Take the time to study the sample maps provided (not to scale) and answer the questions that follow.

There is no time limit to the exercises provided, although you will be under timed conditions during the actual test you will take with the Ambulance Service (if required).

The answers are provided at the end of the exercises.

MAP READING SKILLS EXERCISE 1

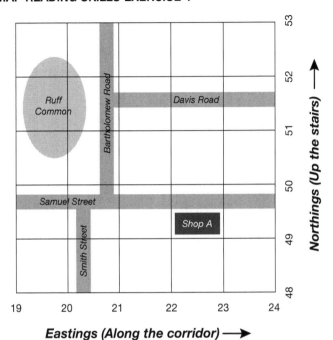

Eastings (Along the corridor) ➔

Study the map above before answering the following questions. Use a 4-figure map reference when giving your answers.

1. The junction of Samuel Street and Smith Street can be found in which grid reference?

Answer [   ]

2. Shop A can be found in which grid reference?

Answer [   ]

3. Which 6 grid references can *'RUFF COMMON'* be found in?

Answer

4. Which grid reference can the junction of Bartholomew Road and Davis Road be found in?

Answer

MAP READING SKILLS EXERCISE 2

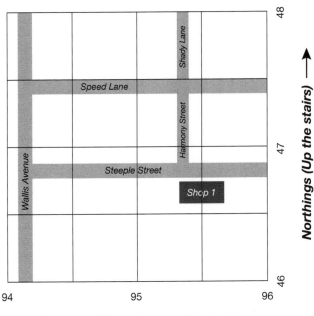

Study the map above before answering the following questions. The map is based on a 6-figure map reference.

1. What is the grid reference at the junction of Wallis Avenue and Steeple Street?

Answer [   ]

2. What can be found at grid reference 955467?

Answer [   ]

3. What is the grid reference at the junction of Steeple Street and Harmony Street?

Answer [   ]

4. What can be found at grid reference 953475?

Answer [   ]

MAP READING SKILLS EXERCISE 3

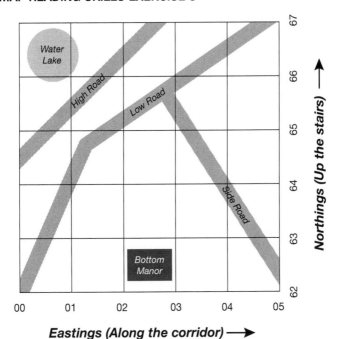

Eastings (Along the corridor) ➔

Study the map above before answering the following questions. The map is based on a 4-figure map reference.

1. Which 3 grid references can Water Lake be found in?

Answer [   ]

2. Which 5 grid references does High Road travel through?

Answer [   ]

3. Which junction can be found in grid reference 0265?

Answer

4. Which grid reference can Bottom Manor be found in?

Answer

MAP READING SKILLS EXERCISE 4

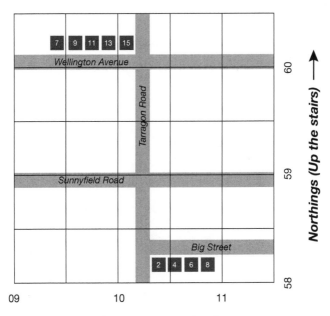

Eastings (Along the corridor) →

Study the map above before answering the following questions. The map is based on a 6-figure map reference.

1. You are called to an incident as a paramedic at number 9, Wellington Avenue. What is the grid reference?

Answer

2. What is the grid reference at the junction of Big Street and Tarragon Road?

Answer

3. What is the grid reference at number 4, Big Street?

Answer [   ]

4. What is located at the grid reference 098602?

Answer [   ]

ANSWERS TO MAP READING SKILLS EXERCISE

Exercise 1

1. 2049

2. 2249

3. 1950; 2050; 1951; 2051; 1952; 2052

4. 2051

Exercise 2

1. 943468

2. Shop 1

3. 953469

4. Junction of Shady Lane and Speed Lane

Exercise 3

1. 0065; 0066; 0166

2. 0064; 0065; 0165; 0166; 0266

3. Junction of Low Road and Side Road

4. 0262

Exercise 4

1. 095602

2. 103583

3. 105582

4. 13, Wellington Avenue

DICTATION/MEMORY TEST

Some NHS trusts may require you to sit a dictation test as part of their application process. The test requires you to read or listen to a given passage, before answering questions on its content. This test assesses your ability to recall information given under timed conditions.

During your paramedic training you will be required to absorb a lot of information and this test is designed to assess your memory and information recalling capability.

On the following pages I have provided you with two exercises to help you prepare for this type of test. Please note that the exercises provided are for practice purposes only and are not the exact tests you will sit on the day.

To begin with, allow yourself two minutes only to read the passage. You are not permitted to take notes. The information contained within each passage relates to the work of a paramedic and will be useful to learn as part of your preparation. Once the two minutes is up, turn over the page and answer the questions. Do not refer back to the information whilst answering the questions.

Once you have finished the first exercise, move on to the next one.

DICTATION/MEMORY TEST EXERCISE 1

Read the following passage for two minutes only before answering the questions on the next page. When answering the questions you are not permitted to refer back to the passage.

The Ambulance Service has undergone a large number of significant changes. In recent years there has been an enormous investment in the training and development of ambulance crews resulting in more effective patient care than ever before.

Every single year hundreds of thousands of people in the United Kingdom will use the Ambulance Service for incidents ranging from heart attacks to broken limbs. Only 10% of the total workload of a typical Ambulance Service is made up by responding to 999 calls. The ambulance crews who make up the emergency response team will usually consist of a fully qualified paramedic and an emergency care assistant. It is their responsibility to ensure that the highest level of patient care is provided to the members of the community in which they serve.

In addition to their emergency work, the Ambulance Service is also involved with additional duties such as Patient Transport Service (PTS).

The paramedics and emergency care assistants whom form part of the ambulance crew are fully competent in their role and can deal with many different types of incidents such as cardiac arrest and road traffic collisions.

In order to carry out their role effectively they will use a wide range of comprehensive equipment such as heart defibrillators, oxygen, intravenous drips, spinal and traction splints, and a variety of drugs for medical and traumatic emergencies.

DICTATION/MEMORY TEST QUESTIONS FOR EXERCISE 1

Question 1

Approximately how many people use the Accident and Emergency Service every year?

Answer

Question 2

In recent years there has been an enormous investment in what?

Answer

Question 3

What percentage of an Ambulance Service's work is taken up by responding to 999 calls?

Answer

Question 4

What does a typical ambulance emergency crew comprise of?

Answer

Question 5

Name 2 different types of equipment that can be found in an ambulance.

Answer

DICTATION/MEMORY TEST ANSWERS FOR EXERCISE 1

Question 1

hundreds of thousands of people.

Question 2

The training and development of ambulance crews.

Question 3

10%

Question 4

A paramedic and an emergency care assistant

Question 5

- Heart defibrillators;

- Oxygen;

- Intravenous drips;

- Spinal and traction splints;

- A variety of drugs for medical and traumatic emergencies.

DICTATION/MEMORY TEST EXERCISE 2

Read the following passage for two minutes only before answering the questions on the following page.

When answering the questions you are not permitted to refer back to the passage.

Non-Emergency Work
The Patient Transport Service (PTS) is a vital part of the Ambulance Service. In basic terms the role of the PTS is to provide transport for a variety of patients such as the following:

- Outpatients;

- Non emergency hospital transfers;

- Those non emergency patients who cannot attend hospital via their own means;

- Routine check ups and appointments;

- Geriatric and psycho-geriatric day care patients.

PTS staff, usually under the role of ambulance care assistants, will crew a specially designed ambulance which has the ability to transport a number of patients in a safe and effective manner. At the rear of the PTS vehicle there will normally be a tail lift which will allow patients to be safely lifted onto, and off the vehicle when required. Ambulance care assistants are trained in the particular needs of the their patients and they will also hold qualifications in first aid, specialist driving skills, patient moving and manual handling techniques, basic life support and patient care skills.

Whilst the role of the PTS does not involve responding to emergency incidents they are crucial to the efficient and

effective running of the Ambulance Service. Without their work the Ambulance Service would not be able to operate.

In some services a number of PTS crews are specially trained as high dependency teams, which are available for patients with specific clinical needs during transport.

DICTATION/MEMORY TEST QUESTIONS FOR EXERCISE 2

Question 1

What does PTS stand for?

Answer

Question 2

Name 2 different types of patients that the PTS transport.

Answer

Question 3

Who are PTS ambulances manned by?

Answer

Question 4

Name two areas that ambulance care assistants are trained in.

Answer

Question 5

The PTS uses vehicles that are fitted with what at the rear?

Answer

DICTATION/MEMORY TEST ANSWERS FOR EXERCISE 2

Question 1

Patient Transport Services.

Question 2

Outpatients, Non emergency hospital transfers, those non emergency patients who cannot attend hospital via their own means, Routine check ups and appointments, Geriatric and psycho-geriatric day care patients.

Question 3

Ambulance care assistants.

Question 4

Ambulance care assistants are trained in the particular needs of the their patients and they will also hold qualifications in first aid, specialist driving skills, patient moving and manual handling techniques, basic life support and patient care skills.

Question 5

Tail lifts.

CHAPTER SEVEN
THE INTERVIEW

Within this section of the guide I have provided you with a large amount of insider tips and advice on how to prepare for the interview. As with any interview, first impressions count for everything.

Try to imagine yourself as the interviewer. How would you expect the person being interviewed to act? What clothes would you expect them to wear? Should they be polite and courteous? Should they be knowledgeable of the role they are applying for, and of the organisation they wish to join? I would hope that the answers to these questions are obvious and they are areas that you should look at carefully during your preparation. Whilst assessing many candidates during interviews for jobs in the emergency services I could always tell those people who had really gone out of their way to prepare. There was a marked difference between them and the other candidates who had carried out a little bit of preparation. Make yourself stand out during the interview for having carried out plenty of research and also be capable

of providing specific examples of life experiences you have gained so far where you can meet the person specification for the role. For example, the role of a paramedic or emergency care assistant requires you to work under pressure whilst following strict guidelines and procedures. Can you think of an example where you have already done this in your current job role, or during your personal life? Try to provide 'specific' examples wherever possible throughout the interview.

Many people spend hours and hours preparing for interviews, usually in the wrong manner. Your approach to your preparation for joining the Ambulance Service should be structured, precise and relevant. Read the pages contained within this guide and in particular the interview questions and responses.

Remember that these are only provided as a guide and are not guaranteed to be the exact questions you will face on the day.

If you would like further help in acquiring competent paramedic interview skills please visit the website www.how2become.com.

AREAS YOU MUST RESEARCH

The number of areas you could research during your preparation for the interview is endless. However, in order to maximise the impact and relevance of your preparation time, I advise that you concentrate on the following areas as a priority:

Learn about the service you are applying to join:

- What does it do?

- How many ambulance stations are there?

- Where are the headquarters and the training centre based?

- Who are the people in charge?

- How many people do they employ?

- What other services do they provide, such as Patient Transport Services?

- Learn and be able to recite the vision/mission statement for the NHS trust.

- Visit your local ambulance station to talk to the crews about the service.

Learn about the role you are applying for:

- What does it involve?

- What qualities are required to perform the role competently?

- What are the duty systems?

- What is the job description?

- How long is the training?

- What does the training involve?

- What are the positive aspects of the role?

- What challenges will you face whilst working as a paramedic or emergency care assistant?

- What skills and experiences do you have that are applicable to the role?

- What are the governing bodies called who set the standard for the role and the training etc?

- What types of equipment would you use whilst working as a paramedic or emergency care assistant?

Visit the website of the service you are applying for:

- Read the Equality scheme and other schemes such as Race, Age, Disability and Gender, Best Practice Statements, Patient Care information, Facts and Figures, Vision Statement and any other relevant information.

Understand Diversity and Community Awareness:

- Be able to explain what the term 'diversity' means and its significance to the role of a paramedic and within the workplace.

- What benefits does a diverse workforce bring to the community?

- Be aware of your local community and its make up. What are the problems in your local community that may cause your problems as a paramedic? How would you overcome these?

During your research you may also wish to read and understand the following bodies and what their role is:

Clinical Governance
Clinical Governance is the Health Service's term for professional self-regulation and accountability. In order to achieve Clinical Governance each NHS trust will be required to comply with auditing and quality assurance procedures. The NHS defines Clinical Governance as: 'A framework through which NHS organisations are accountable for continuously improving the quality of their services and safeguarding high standards of care by creating an environment in which excellence in clinical care will flourish.'

Health Professions Council
The Health Professions Council is currently the body to which paramedics in the UK are currently registered (as of April

2002). It is now the law that UK Ambulance Services only employ registered paramedics. It is also against the law for anyone not registered with the Health Professions Council to call themselves a 'paramedic'. The Health Professions Council used to be called the Council for Professions Supplementary to Medicine (CPSM).

Website: www.hpc-uk.org

Community Safety Partnerships

The title or name of these partnerships is constantly changing in order to meet the needs of the community. In very basic terms this type of partnership involves local stakeholders, such as the Ambulance Service, Fire Service, Police Force and other such relevant parties, coming together in a forum to discuss the problems they may face within the community. They use a collective approach in order to tackle crime and also to make the community a safer place. This will also be the appropriate forum for the ambulance Service to discuss their problems or concerns with issues that directly affect them – for example, alcohol related issues and incidents within a town or city centre.

EDEXCEL

EDEXCEL is the government body who will monitor and oversee all training standards for paramedics and other associated roles in the UK. It is also the body that will issue your qualification once you become a qualified paramedic.

Website: www.edexcel.com

Operational Research Consultancy (ORCON)

This is the National body that is responsible for creating and monitoring the response time targets for the UK Ambulance Service. Response time targets are revised from time to time.

Professional Advisory Group (PAG)

The Professional Advisory Group are a group of professional health care personnel who are responsible for advising Ambulance Services on patient care procedures and other associated issues. They are usually doctors or other health care practitioners with the appropriate experience and/ or qualifications.

United Kingdom Resuscitation Council (UKRC)

The aim of this body is to research and promote best known practice in resuscitation care.

Joint Royal Colleges Ambulance Liaison Committee (JRCALC)

The role of the JRCALC is to provide special clinical advice to the Ambulance Services. As part of its role It will produce regularly updated Clinical Practice Guidelines and issue them to each NHS trust Ambulance Service.

Website: jrcalc.org.uk

During your research, and also whilst visiting your local ambulance station, you may also become aware of other relevant bodies and organisations that will assist you in your preparation. I would advise that you just be aware that they exist, and what their main roles are, rather than spending hours and hours learning about each organisation of body.

RESPONDING TO SITUATIONAL INTEVIEW QUESTIONS

Situational interview questions are extremely common during the paramedic and emergency care assistant selection interview. This type of questioning requires you to provide examples of where you have already been in a specific situation in the past and demonstrated certain skills and attributes. For example, as a paramedic you will often be required to work under pressure whilst performing difficult

tasks. Therefore the interview panel may ask you a question along the following lines:

"Can you provide an example of where you have carried out a difficult task whilst under pressure from other people?"

In order to answer the question effectively you must provide an example of where you have already demonstrated these skills. More importantly, your answer must be 'specific' in nature. A specific response means that you must provide an example of where you have actually been in this type of situation before. Do not fall into the trap of providing a 'generic' response that details what you 'would do' if the situation arose.

It is also important that you structure your responses in a logical and concise manner. The way to achieve this is to use the 'STAR' method of interview question response construction:

Situation

Start off your response to the interview question by explaining what the 'situation' was and who was involved.

Task

Once you have detailed the situation, explain what the 'task' was, or what needed to be done.

Action

Now explain what 'action' you took, and what action others took. Also explain why you took this particular course of action.

Result

Explain what the outcome or result was following your actions and those of others. Try to demonstrate in your response that the result was positive because of the action you took.

Finally, explain to the panel what you would do differently if the same situation arose again. It is good to be reflective at the end of your responses. This demonstrates a level of maturity and it will also show the panel that you are willing to learn from every experience.

MAKING A FIRST IMPRESSION

"You only get one chance to make a first impression" – A brief but true statement!

As soon as you walk into the interview room, the panel will formulate an opinion of you within 10 seconds; so make sure you follow these guidelines:

- Be smart and well turned out – smart suit, shirt and tie (for men), clean shoes, tidy and neat hair;

- Smile and introduce yourself;

- Don't sit down until invited to do so;

- Don't slouch in the interview chair but instead sit upright and keep your hands faced downwards on your knees;

- Make sure that you are FULLY prepared and have learnt everything you can about the role you are applying for and the organisation you are trying to join;

- Be positive about their service – try to find out positive things that the service has achieved or been a part of, and mention these in your responses;

- Make sure you have read your application form the day before the interview as you may be asked questions on your responses.

SAMPLE INTERVIEW QUESTIONS

The type of interview questions you will be asked by the panel will very much depend on the service or trust you are applying to join. However, the interview will predominantly be based around the following areas:

- The application form and your responses;
- The reasons why you want to join their Ambulance Service;
- What you know about their Ambulance Service;
- What you know about the role you are applying for and the qualities required performing it competently;
- Your skills, experiences and qualifications that relate to the role;
- What you think the job involves;
- How you deal with difficult situations;
- Your knowledge and understanding of diversity and community awareness;
- What the training involves in order to successfully qualify in the role.

The interview will normally be carried out by two people, depending on the service you are applying to join. For example, some Ambulance Services will use a human resources officer and a duty station officer to carry out the interview, which will last up to one hour in duration.

On the following pages I have provided a number of sample interview questions and responses. The responses I have provided are for illustration purposes only and they should not be used during your own interview. Be sure to create responses to the questions based on your own skills and experiences.

SAMPLE INTERVIEW QUESTION NUMBER 1

Why do you want to join this particular Ambulance Service and what do you have to offer?

This type of question is extremely common so your response should be prepared beforehand. The type of information you provide in your response needs to focus on the job description and the vision statement of the particular service you are applying to join. Remember that the Ambulance Service is exactly that – 'a service'.

The London Ambulance Service's vision is as follows – 'A world-class ambulance service for London staffed by well-trained, enthusiastic and proud people who are all recognised for contributing to the provision of high-quality patient care'. Look at the vision statement of the service you are applying to join and you will find some useful tips here to help you structure your response.

On the following page I have provided you with a sample response to this question. Read the example provided and then use the template provided to create your own.

SAMPLE RESPONSE TO INTERVIEW QUESTION NUMBER 1

Why do you want to join this particular Ambulance Service and what do you have to offer?

"I have always been interested in this type of work, where caring for the needs of others is a priority. I understand that the job is demanding and stressful at times but the satisfaction of working in a close knit team that helps others in need is something that very much appeals to me.

Having looked into this particular service, I am impressed by the standards it sets itself. I am a self-disciplined, trusted and enthusiastic person who would thrive in such a role, where serving our diverse community is its main aim.

My previous experience of working in a customer-based role has given me a good foundation for this type of work. I have experience of dealing with difficult situations and have the maturity and ability to diffuse conflict situations when the need arises.

I am hard working, reliable and committed in everything I do and believe I would be a great asset to your already successful team. I also keep myself physically fit and active and understand that the role of emergency medical technician is demanding.

Finally, I have read and understand the vision statement of this Ambulance Service. I believe I have the commitment and motivation to abide by these important standards and would very much thrive in a professional organisation where teamwork and self discipline are of great importance."

TEMPLATE FOR INTERVIEW QUESTION NUMBER 1

Why do you want to join this particular Ambulance Service and what do you have to offer?

SAMPLE INTERVIEW QUESTION NUMBER 2

What do you imagine will be the best bits about the job?

This type of question is designed to test your knowledge of the job you are applying for. When responding to this type of question, you should try to focus on the wider picture as opposed to saying things like:

'Driving to calls in the ambulance with the bells and lights going'

'The laughs that I'll have with my colleagues'

'The pay, leave and benefits'

Instead, you should concentrate on areas such as the job satisfaction of helping others in the community, working in a close-knit and well-trained team etc. With questions of this nature you will start to appreciate the importance of a station visit or ride out. The crews will be able to tell you exactly what the best parts of the job are. Make sure that your response to this question is sensible and professional. I have now provided you with a sample response to this type of question. Read it, and then use the ideas contained within it to create your own response based on your own views and opinions.

SAMPLE RESPONSE TO INTERVIEW QUESTION NUMBER 2

What do you imagine will be the best bits about the job?

"During my research I was fortunate enough to visit my local ambulance station in order to gain some valuable information and advice about their role.

I believe the most rewarding aspect would be saving someone's life. Although you do not want people to become ill or get injured it is a fact that they do, so being able to help them and care for them must be very rewarding. Knowing that you've worked hard to pass your exams and are working to the best of your ability must also be a fantastic feeling.

I imagine that working in a close-knit, professional and well-respected organisation must give you a great sense of pride. I would definitely feel proud to be working for this Ambulance Service.

Working with the other emergency services would also be a great part of the job. I imagine that you have to work closely with them on a daily basis so the relationship between the services must be quite strong and enjoyable.

Above all, working in and caring for the community would be the most enjoyable part of the job. I imagine you must get to meet a wide range of people from different backgrounds and cultures. I would look forward to interacting with and meeting different people from the community that I served in."

TEMPLATE FOR INTERVIEW QUESTION NUMBER 2

What do you imagine will be the best bits about the job?

SAMPLE INTERVIEW QUESTION NUMBER 3

What do you imagine will be the worst bits about the job?

This type of question again is designed to test your knowledge of the job you are applying for.

During your visit to the ambulance station the crews will be able to provide you with details about the aspects of the job that are testing and difficult. When responding to questions of this nature make sure you are professional and always steer away from any negative personal views and opinions that relate to how the trust is run. For example, if the trust has received some bad publicity in relation to attendance times for example, it is wise not to build your response based around media coverage and public opinion, as these are often wrong and do not provide the full facts.

I have now provided you with a sample response to this type of question. Read it, and then use the ideas contained within it to create your own individual response using the template provided.

SAMPLE RESPONSE TO INTERVIEW QUESTION NUMBER 3

What do you imagine will be the worst bits about the job?

"Not being able to reach somebody in time must be quite frustrating, especially if you are stuck in traffic and other road users aren't helping the situation. I often see my local ambulance trying to respond to incidents and the traffic in front of them is not moving out of the way. I imagine you must have to stay calm in those situations and try to get there as quickly as possible.

I understand that you have to deal with conflict and sometimes members of the public who are aggressive or under the influence of alcohol. These situations must test your professionalism but being able to remain calm under pressure and diffuse difficult situations is all part of the role.

Finally, I would imagine that hoax calls are extremely frustrating. Ambulances are there for those who need them the most but unfortunately people still make hoax calls. It must be terrible when you are responding to a hoax call when somebody else at the other end of town genuinely needs your help."

TEMPLATE FOR INTERVIEW QUESTION NUMBER 3

What do you imagine will be the worst bits about the job?

SAMPLE INTERVIEW QUESTION NUMBER 4

Give an example of where you have had to deal with a member of the public in a potential conflict situation (violent, drunk, angry etc). How did you attempt to take control of the situation?

This type of question is designed to assess your emotional maturity and assertiveness. Whilst working as a paramedic or emergency care assistant you may face difficult situations where some members of the public are under the influence of alcohol and acting in a violent manner. When answering this type of question you must give a response that demonstrates how you have dealt with similar situations in the past. It will not be good enough just to tell them how you 'would' deal with this situation if it arose but moreover how you 'have' dealt with this type of situation in the past.

I have now provided you with a sample response to this type of question. Read it first before preparing your own response using the template provided.

SAMPLE RESPONSE TO INTERVIEW QUESTION NUMBER 4

Give an example of where you have had to deal with a member of the public in a potential conflict situation (violent, drunk, angry etc). How did you attempt to take control of the situation?

"Whilst working in my current role as a customer service manager I was faced with an angry customer who was dissatisfied with the level of service he had received from our shop. He had purchased a pair of shoes for his daughter's birthday but when she went to open the shoes she found that they were both of a different size. The shop assistant had made a mistake and should have checked the shoe sizes before selling them to the gentleman.

Unfortunately, when I tried to apologise for our error and offer a full refund along with a new pair of shoes for his daughter, he refused to calm down and continued to act in an angry manner.

I knew that it was important for me to remain calm and not respond to his aggression. If I had responded in a similar aggressive manner I would have been making the situation worse, so I decided to stay calm and talk to him in a mild-mannered voice, asking him politely not to shout at me.

Unfortunately, he did not calm down. Instead, he began to swear and threaten me, suggesting that the member of staff who made the mistake should be sacked immediately and if I didn't do this, I would be in trouble. I then decided to give him a warning that if he didn't calm down and stop swearing, the Police would be called. He did not listen to me, so I walked away from the confrontational situation and telephoned the Police.

As soon as he saw me calling the Police the man left the shop. Although he had left the shop I still asked for the Police to attend due to the threatening behaviour.

When the Police arrived I gave a statement and requested that the matter be investigated.

I believe it is important to provide an excellent level of service to our customers but that does not mean that you should accept any form of verbal or physical abuse. I would never respond aggressively to any such situation. Instead I would always walk away from a situation like this and inform the relevant authorities."

TEMPLATE FOR INTERVIEW QUESTION NUMBER 4

Give an example of where you have had to deal with a member of the public in a potential conflict situation (violent, drunk, angry etc). How did you attempt to take control of the situation?

SAMPLE INTERVIEW QUESTION NUMBER 5

What different tactics might you use to avoid a confrontational situation?

This type of question is designed to assess your ability to diffuse potentially difficult and confrontational situations.

Always remember that, whilst you should be assertive, it is unacceptable to become aggressive or confrontational yourself. This will just make the situation worse and do nothing to diffuse the situation. You must also have the common sense to realise that when a situation is becoming dangerous you need to walk away and protect both yourself and your colleagues.

Whilst working as a paramedic or emergency care assistant you will be dealing with people who are under the influence of alcohol and therefore have the potential to become aggressive. When responding to these types of question try to show your knowledge of different tactics that can be employed to diffuse confrontational situations. It is worth mentioning that you will use the training that you are given by the Ambulance Service to avoid confrontational situations.

Use the sample response that follows to assist you in preparing your own based on your own views and opinions.

SAMPLE RESPONSE TO INTERVIEW QUESTION NUMBER 5

What different tactics might you use to avoid a confrontational situation?

"To begin with, probably the most important factor is to remember not to respond in a similar, confrontational manner. This will only make the situation worse.

I believe it is important not to be intimidated by such behaviour and there is a level of assertiveness that must be applied. I would try to talk to the individual in a calm manner, trying to establish a rapport with them. I would ask them what their name was and ask them some questions to try to diffuse the situation. I would try to use both verbal and non-verbal communication skills to avoid a confrontational situation including body language that is non-aggressive. I would listen to what they were saying and try to verbally intervene at an appropriate time, asking questions about how they felt and calling them by their first name if possible.

If I could get the person to sit down and try to relax this would help to diffuse the situation. Talking to them in a calm manner is important. However, if I were unable to diffuse a confrontational situation, I would know when to walk away and ask for assistance.

The safety of myself and my work colleagues is paramount."

TEMPLATE FOR INTERVIEW QUESTION NUMBER 5

What different tactics might you use to avoid a confrontational situation?

SAMPLE INTERVIEW QUESTION NUMBER 6

Some people think we should treat everyone the same, others say we should treat everyone differently. What do you think?

This type of question is designed to test your ability to interact effectively with people from diverse backgrounds.

To begin with, you need to understand what diversity is and the benefits it brings to our society and the workplace. Do you know the benefits? The community in which we live in is diverse in nature. Our community is diverse in terms of its racial, ethnic, gender, cultural, disability, sexual orientation, and social differences. Diversity brings many positive things to society. In order for the Ambulance Service to provide a high level of service to the public it serves then it needs to be representative of society.

The Amendment to the 1976 Race Relations Act places a new statutory duty on all public bodies, including the Ambulance Service, to positively promote race equality in service delivery and employment.

Each NHS trust is required to produce a Race Equality Scheme, and other equality schemes such as age, gender and disability. It would be worth reading the Equality Schemes of the service you are applying to join before you attend the interview. Although you are unlikely to be asked questions on their specific content it would be good to have knowledge of their existence. If you do make reference to any of them during your interview, make sure you understand what you are talking about! When responding to this type of question you need to demonstrate your knowledge of diversity and the positive aspects it brings to our society and the workplace. Take a look at the following response before constructing your own using the template on the next page.

SAMPLE RESPONSE TO INTERVIEW QUESTION NUMBER 6

Some people think we should treat everyone the same, others say we should treat everyone differently. What do you think?

"I believe we should treat everybody with respect and dignity and in a manner that is appropriate to their needs. Our community is diverse in nature, which brings many positive aspects to society. Just because somebody is from a different background or culture doesn't mean to say they should be treated any differently or have a different level of service.

Everybody in the community should receive the same care and treatment regardless of their race, gender, age, sexual orientation or disabilities. It is important that, as a public service, we understand our community and respond to its needs. Our community is diverse and therefore we need to understand and respect the people within it.

I have already read the Race Equality Scheme for the Service and I have tried to understand what it means and how it impacts on the Ambulance Service."

TEMPLATE FOR INTERVIEW QUESTION NUMBER 6

Some people think we should treat everyone the same, others say we should treat everyone differently. What do you think?

SAMPLE INTERVIEW QUESTION NUMBER 7

Why do you think the Ambulance Service puts so much importance upon diversity and community awareness?

This type of question is again looking to assess your ability to interact effectively with people from diverse backgrounds.

In order to provide the highest level of service, a public service such as the Ambulance Service must be as diverse as the community in which it serves.

Once again, it is advisable to be aware of the Race Equality Scheme for the service you are applying to join.

The Ambulance Service must understand the needs of its community in order to provide the highest level of service. This can only be achieved through a process of continuous development and learning. By interacting with the community and responding to its needs, the Ambulance Service will continue to improve and develop.

Make sure you understand the importance of diversity, but more importantly believe in it! Use the sample response that follows to assist you in preparing your own based on your own views and opinions.

SAMPLE RESPONSE TO INTERVIEW QUESTION NUMBER 7

Why do you think the Ambulance Service puts so much importance upon diversity and community awareness?

"For the simple reason that the community in which it serves is diverse in nature and therefore requires a service that is both understanding, culturally aware, responsive to its needs and willing to learn.

If the community in which we live is diverse, then the public services that represent it should be too. In terms of community awareness, the Ambulance Service must understand the needs of the community in which it serves.

It should be aware of the different cultures and backgrounds of its community, so that it can be respectful and understand the needs of everyone in society. By doing this it will be able to provide the highest level of service to the people it serves.

If the Ambulance Service is not aware of the community it cares for then it cannot continually improve and provide the highest level of service to everyone."

TEMPLATE FOR INTERVIEW QUESTION NUMBER 7

Why do you think the Ambulance Service puts so much importance upon diversity and community awareness?

SAMPLE INTERVIEW QUESTION NUMBER 8

Can you provide an example of when you have worked as part of a team to achieve a goal?

Having the ability to work as part of a team is very important to the role of a paramedic and emergency care assistant. Ambulance Services employ many people in different roles, from 999 call operators to vehicle mechanics to administrative workers. In fact, it is not uncommon for thousands of people to work for one particular service. As an example, there are over 4000 people working for the London Ambulance Service! Therefore, it is essential that every member of the team works together in order to achieve the ultimate goal of providing a high quality level of patient care.

The recruitment staff will want to be certain that you can work effectively as part of a team, which is why you may be asked questions that relate to your team-working experience. Not only should you be capable of working effectively with other paramedics but also with other workers within the service and outside of it. There now follows a sample response to this question. Once you have read it, take time to construct your own response using the template provided.

SAMPLE RESPONSE TO INTERVIEW QUESTION NUMBER 8

Can you provide an example of when you have worked as part of a team to achieve a goal?

"Yes, I can. I like to keep fit and healthy and as part of this aim I play football for a local Sunday team. We had worked very hard to get to the cup final and we were faced with playing a very good opposition team who had recently won the league title. After only ten minutes of play, one of our players was sent off and we conceded a penalty as a result. Being one goal down and 80 minutes left to play we were faced with a mountain to climb.

However, we all remembered our training and worked very hard in order to prevent any more goals being scored. Due to playing with ten players, I had to switch positions and play as a defender, something that I am not used to. The team worked brilliantly to hold off any further opposing goals and after 60 minutes we managed to get an equaliser. The game went to penalties in the end and we managed to win the cup.

I believe I am an excellent team player and can always be relied upon to work as an effective team member at all times. I understand that being an effective team member is very important if the Ambulance Service is to provide a high level of service to the community that it serves. Part of the role of a paramedic includes working with other teams, both within the service and also outside it, such as the Police and Fire Service."

TEMPLATE FOR INTERVIEW QUESTION NUMBER 8

Can you provide an example of when you have worked as part of a team to achieve a goal?

SAMPLE INTERVIEW QUESTION NUMBER 9

Can you provide an example of a situation when you have had to work under pressure?

The role of a paramedic will often require you to work under extreme pressure. Therefore, the recruitment staff will want to know that you have the ability to perform in such an environment. If you already have experience of working under pressure then you are far more likely to succeed as a paramedic and be capable of meeting the demands of the job.

When responding to a question of this nature, try to provide an actual example of where you have achieved a task whilst being under pressure. Don't forget to follow the guidance at the beginning of this section, which related to responding effectively to 'situational' interview questions. Questions of this nature are sometimes included in the application form, so try to use a different example for the interview, if the question comes up.

There now follows a sample response to this question. Once you have read it, take the time to construct your own response based on your own individual experiences and knowledge and using the template provided.

SAMPLE RESPONSE TO INTERVIEW QUESTION NUMBER 9

Can you provide an example of a situation when you have had to work under pressure?

"Yes, I can. In my current job as car mechanic for a well-known company, I was presented with a difficult and pressurised situation. A member of the team had made a mistake and had fitted a number of wrong components to a car. The car in question was due to be picked up at 2pm and the customer had stated how important it was that his car was ready on time because he had an important meeting to attend.

We only had two hours in which to resolve the issue and I volunteered to be the one who would carry out the work on the car. The problem was that we had 3 other customers in the workshop waiting for their cars too, so I was the only person who could be spared at that particular time. I worked solidly for the next 2 hours, making sure that I meticulously carried out each task in line with our operating procedures.

Even though I didn't finish the car until 2.10pm, I managed to achieve a very difficult task under pressurised conditions whilst following strict procedures and regulations. I understand that the role of a paramedic will require me to work under extreme pressure at times and I believe I have the experience to achieve this. I am very meticulous in my work and always ensure that I take personal responsibility to keep up to date with procedures and policies in my current job."

TEMPLATE FOR INTERVIEW QUESTION NUMBER 9

Can you provide an example of a situation when you have had to work under pressure?

SAMPLE INTERVIEW QUESTION NUMBER 10

What skills do you possess that you think would be an asset to our organisation?

When responding to questions of this nature, try to match your skills with the skills that are required of a paramedic. On some Ambulance Service websites you will be able to read about the type of person they are looking to employ, usually in the recruitment section. An example of this would be:

'We are looking for highly organised and caring team players who are of a compassionate disposition. You will possess a good level of manual dexterity and be capable of upholding the principles of our organisation whilst providing a high level of patient care to the people whom we serve.'

Just by looking at the Ambulance Service's website, you should be able to obtain some clues as to the type of person they are seeking to employ. It is also worthwhile studying the job description and person specification, as these will also provide details of the type of person they are looking to employ. Try to think of the skills that are required to perform the role you are applying for and include them in your response.

There now follows a sample response to this question. Once you have read it, take the time to construct your own response using the template provided.

SAMPLE RESPONSE TO INTERVIEW QUESTION NUMBER 10

What skills do you possess that you think would be an asset to our organisation?

"I am a very conscientious person who takes the time to learn and develop new skills correctly. I have vast experience working in a customer-focused environment and fully understand that excellent patient care is important. It is important that every member of the team works towards providing a high level of service. I believe I have the skills, knowledge and experience to do this. I am a very good team player and can always be relied upon to carry out my role to the highest of standards. I am a flexible person and understand that there is a need to be available at short notice to cover duties if required. In addition to these skills and attributes, I am a very good communicator and understand that different members of the community will need a different approach. For example, when dealing with elderly members of the community I will have to be very patient and cater for their needs in a more sensitive manner.

I am highly safety conscious and have a health and safety qualification to my name. Therefore, I can be relied upon to perform all procedures correctly and in line with my training and will not put others or myself in any danger whatsoever.

Finally, I am very good at learning new skills, which means that I will work hard to pass all of my continuation training if I am successful in becoming a paramedic."

TEMPLATE FOR INTERVIEW QUESTION NUMBER 10

What skills do you possess that you think would be an asset to our organisation?

SAMPLE INTERVIEW QUESTION NUMBER 11

What can you tell us about the role of a paramedic/ emergency care assistant?

You must be well prepared for this question prior to your interview. If you don't know what the role involves, then you shouldn't be applying for the post. When responding to this question, make sure you make reference to the job/person specification for the role. The job specification is a 'blueprint' for the role you will be required to perform whilst working as a paramedic. Therefore, it is essential that you know it. An example of a job description for a paramedic is detailed below:

Sample job description

Paramedics are required to work in rapid response ambulance units to deal with medical emergencies and incidents. These emergencies may include minor injuries, illness, and casualties that arise from road and rail accidents, criminal violence, fires and other incidents. Paramedics are usually the first healthcare professionals on the scene and they assess the patient's condition and initiate specialist medical treatment and care before admission to hospital. The primary goal of paramedics is to meet people's immediate treatment needs. They resuscitate and stabilise patients by using advanced life support techniques, administer drips, drugs and oxygen, and apply splints, and also assist with complex hospital transfers.

Before you prepare a response to this question, you will need to obtain a copy of the job description/person specification for the role that you are applying for. Now take a look at the following response before constructing your own response using the template provided.

SAMPLE RESPONSE TO INTERVIEW QUESTION NUMBER 11

What can you tell us about the role of a paramedic?

"I understand that the role involves a high level of responsibility, concentration and the ability to work under pressure. To begin with, paramedics are required to work in rapid response ambulance units to deal with medical emergencies and incidents. These emergencies may include minor injuries, illness, and casualties that arise from road and rail accidents, criminal violence, fires and other incidents. Paramedics are usually the first healthcare professionals on the scene and they assess the patient's condition and initiate specialist medical treatment and care before admission to hospital.

During incidents, paramedics are required to assess the condition of patients who are injured or taken ill suddenly. Once that initial assessment has been carried out, they will need to decide what action is needed and then initiate any appropriate treatment following policies and procedures.

Paramedics will also have to deal with members of the public and family members who are present at the scene with a view to calming them down and reassuring them using effective communication techniques.

In addition to their operational duties, they must ensure their equipment is fully serviceable and operational. There will be a large degree of training and they must also keep up to date with policies, rules and procedures so that they can maintain their high standard of patient care. Finally, paramedics will need to be able to work with their community and other external stakeholders such as the Police and Fire Service with a view to working together to reduce incidents and thus make the community a safer place to live."

TEMPLATE FOR INTERVIEW QUESTION NUMBER 11

What can you tell us about the role of a paramedic?

SAMPLE INTERVIEW QUESTION NUMBER 12

Why do you want to work for this particular Ambulance Service?

Once again this is a question that is likely to come up during your interview.

In order to prepare for this question, you need to carry out some research about the Ambulance Service. The best place to get this information is via their website and also within your application pack and recruitment literature.

When responding to this type of question, try to focus on the positive aspects of the service's work. Do they run any community based initiatives or have they won any awards for the high standard of care they provide? It is always good to make reference to the positive aspects of their work, but do not mention any current or previous bad press or publicity.

There now follows a sample response to this question to help you prepare. Once you have read it, take the time to construct your own answer using the template provided.

SAMPLE RESPONSE TO INTERVIEW QUESTION NUMBER 12

Why do you want to work for this particular Ambulance Service?

"Having studied your website, the recruitment literature and also visited my local Ambulance Station, I have been impressed with the professionalism, commitment and dedication of what I have seen and heard.

When I visited the ambulance station the crews were busy preparing for a joint emergency services training exercise by way of a tabletop exercise. I was intrigued to see the level of preparation that they were putting into this event and I would love to be part of a well-organised and disciplined team.

I have noticed on your website that you are promoting a number of initiatives that are designed to improve the health and well being of the people in the community. This is particularly impressive as it demonstrates that the service is very much proactive and not just a reactive organisation. Personally I am a well-organised and disciplined person who maintains high standards, so I strongly believe that I would be a great asset to this trust. I have not applied to any other service, as I believe this one is the only one I want to work for.

Finally, all of the people I have met during my research have been very helpful and they have all gone out of their way to assist me. I think this says a tremendous amount about the quality of people you have within the organisation and I would very much like to be a part of this team."

TEMPLATE FOR INTERVIEW QUESTION NUMBER 12

Why do you want to work for this particular Ambulance Service?

SAMPLE INTERVIEW QUESTION NUMBER 13

Why do you want to become a paramedic/emergency care assistant?

This question is inevitable, so it is important that you ensure you have a suitable answer prepared. Many people will respond with a standard answer such as – "It's something that I've always wanted do since I was young". Whilst this is ok, you need to back it up with genuine reasons that relate to the role and also the Ambulance Service that you are applying to join. Try to think of more positive reasons for wanting to be a paramedic such as:

- Working in a customer-focused environment;

- A genuine desire to learn new skills;

- The opportunity to make a difference to the community;

- The chance to work with highly professional people;

- The challenges that the role will bring.

This type of question may be posed in a number of different formats such as the following:

- Why do you want to become a paramedic with our Trust?

- What has attracted you to the role of paramedic?

There now follows a sample response to help you prepare for this type of question. Once you have read it, use the template provided to create your own response based upon your own views and opinions.

SAMPLE RESPONSE TO INTERVIEW QUESTION NUMBER 13

Why do you want to become a paramedic/emergency care assistant?

"I have wanted to become a paramedic for many years now. Approximately 5 years ago the local ambulance crew visited my university to give a careers presentation. During the presentation I began to realise that the skills required to become a paramedic were suited to my abilities and experience. It was then that I began to prepare for the job by embarking on a number of educational courses that would prepare me for the role.

In addition to this I have always had the urge to work in a job where you have the ability to make a positive difference. I am a practical person who very much enjoys working with other people and I want to do a job that is worthwhile and respected in society. I set myself high standards and I want to work in a career where you need to be organised, disciplined and focused on the job in hand.

Finally, whilst I am more than capable of working on my own and unsupervised, I want to work as part of a team. Throughout my life I have worked in many different teams and I enjoy getting tasks and jobs done whilst working with others."

TEMPLATE FOR INTERVIEW QUESTION NUMBER 13

Why do you want to become a paramedic/emergency care assistant?

SAMPLE INTERVIEW QUESTION NUMBER 14

Can you provide us with an example of a safety-related task that you have had to perform?

Safety is an extremely important part of the paramedic's role, and the recruitment staff need to know that you are capable of working safely at all times. The term 'safety' should be an integral part of your responses during the interview. Making reference to the fact that you are aware of the importance of safety is a positive thing.

When responding to safety-related questions you should try to include examples where you have had to work to, or follow, safety guidelines or procedures. If you have a safety qualification then it is definitely worthwhile mentioning this during your interview. Any relevant safety experience or safety-related role should also be discussed.

Now take a look at the sample response before using the provided template to construct your own response.

SAMPLE RESPONSE TO INTERVIEW QUESTION NUMBER 14

Can you provide us with an example of a safety-related task that you have had to perform?

"I currently work as a gas fitter and I am often required to perform safety-related tasks. An example of one of these tasks would involve the installation of gas-fired boilers. When fitting a gas boiler, I have to ensure that I carry out a number of safety checks during the installation stage, which ensures my work is safe and to a high standard.

In addition to carrying out work in line with procedures and regulations, I also carry out daily checks on my equipment to ensure that it is serviceable, operational and safe. If I find any problems then I immediately take steps to get the equipment repaired by a qualified engineer or technician.

I have been trained, and I am qualified, to carry out my work in accordance with strict safety guidelines. I also have a number of safety certificates to demonstrate my competence.

I am fully aware that if I do not carry out my job in accordance with safety guidelines there is the possibility that somebody may be injured or even killed."

TEMPLATE FOR INTERVIEW QUESTION NUMBER 14

Can you provide us with an example of a safety-related task that you have had to perform?

FURTHER SAMPLE GENERIC INTERVIEW QUESTIONS

Now that we have completed studying the types of possible interview questions you may be asked, I will provide you with a number of generic interview questions that you may be asked during the paramedic interview.

Please note I have not provided sample responses to these questions, as the response you provide must be solely based around your own skills, knowledge and experience.

SAMPLE GENERIC INTERVIEW QUESTION NUMBER 1

Can you provide us with an example of when you have had to work in an emergency?

This question is also likely to be asked during the application form stage of the process. Being able to remain calm under pressure is very important and will form an integral part of your training. Maybe you have had to deal with an emergency at work or even in the home?

Whatever example you decide to use, make sure you tell the interviewers that you stayed calm and focused on the task in hand. Make reference to the importance of safety during your response too.

SAMPLE GENERIC INTERVIEW QUESTION NUMBER 2

Do you think you would get bored of routine tasks such as checking your equipment and reading up on procedures etc?

Of course the only answer here is no. Part of the job of a paramedic and emergency care assistant is to check and familiarise yourself with your equipment and keep up to

date with procedures. Every job has mundane tasks but it is usually these tasks that are the most important.

SAMPLE GENERIC INTERVIEW QUESTION NUMBER 3

How many people work for this organisation and where are the ambulance stations located?

Questions that relate to facts and figures or the structure of the service are commonplace. The panel will want to know that you are serious about joining their Ambulance Service and that you have looked into their organisation in detail. Make sure you study the organisation, the people and its structure before you attend the interview. You will be able to find plenty of information on the service's website.

SAMPLE GENERIC INTERVIEW QUESTION NUMBER 4

What are the vision/mission and aims of this company?

Many organisations, including Ambulance Services and NHS Trusts, set themselves aims and objectives. They will also have a vision or mission statement and a patient charter. These usually relate to the high level of customer service and patient care that they promise to deliver. When you apply to become a paramedic or emergency care assistant you should study these important documents and be able to recite them. It will look good in your interview if you can explain in detail what these involve. Learning this kind of information is important and it will put you ahead of the competition.

Always remember this rule – Working for the Trust comes first, becoming a paramedic comes second! Visit the website of the Trust in order to view their mission, aims, objectives or patient charter.

SAMPLE GENERIC INTERVIEW QUESTION NUMBER 5

How do you think you would cope with working under strenuous conditions for long periods of time?

Paramedics are often required to work under difficult conditions for lengthy periods of time. You will attend many road traffic collisions during your time, where your skills, stamina and professionalism will be tested to the limit. Can you cope with it? Do you have any experience of working under these types of conditions? If you do have experiences in this area then try to provide an example when responding to this question.

SAMPLE GENERIC INTERVIEW QUESTION NUMBER 6

What is your sickness record like and what do you think is an acceptable level of sickness?

The Ambulance Service wants to employ people who have good sickness records. Your attendance at work is integral to the smooth running of the ambulance station. When you go off work sick, it affects the other team members, as somebody will have to cover. Basically no amount of sickness is acceptable but obviously genuine sickness cannot be helped. Remember to tell the panel that you do not take time off sick unless absolutely necessary and you can be relied upon to come to work.

SAMPLE GENERIC INTERVIEW QUESTION NUMBER 7

Have you ever worked during the night and how do you feel about working shifts?

The work of a paramedic involves irregular shift patterns and the Ambulance Service will want to know that you can handle

them. Speak to any person who works shifts and they will tell you that after a number of years they can start to take their toll. Remember to tell the panel that you are looking forward to working shifts and, in particular, night duties. If you can provide examples of where you have worked irregular shift patterns then remember to tell them as this will work in your favour. It may also be advisable to tell the panel that your family fully support you in your application and they appreciate the impact working shifts may have on your home and social life.

SAMPLE GENERIC INTERVIEW QUESTION NUMBER 8

Can you provide us with an example of a project you have had to complete and the obstacles you had to overcome?

Having the ability to complete tasks and projects successfully demonstrates that you have the ability to complete your paramedic/ambulance technician training.

Many people give up on things in life and they fail to achieve their goals. The recruitment staff will want to know that you are going to complete all of your training successfully and, if you can provide evidence of where you have already done this, then this will go in your favour.

When responding to this type of question, try to think of a difficult, long drawn-out task that you achieved despite a number of obstacles that were in your way.

FURTHER TIPS AND ADVICE FOR PREPARING FOR THE PARAMEDIC INTERVIEW

- The interviewers may ask you more generic questions relating to your past experiences or skills. These may be in relation to how you solve problems, your strengths and weaknesses, team-working skills, communication skills and questions that relate to the physical aspects of the role. Make sure you have examples for each of these.

- Try to speak to a current serving paramedic or emergency care assistant of the service that you are applying to join. Ask him/her what it is like to work for that particular service and what current issues they are facing.

- Try to think of a time when you have made a mistake and how you learnt from the experience. The panel may ask you questions that relate to how you deal with setbacks in your life.

- When you complete the application form, make sure you keep a copy of it. Before you go to your interview ensure that you read the application form over and over again as you may find you are asked questions about your responses.

- Don't be afraid to ask the interviewer to repeat a question if you do not hear it the first time. Take your time when answering and be measured in your responses.

- If you don't know the answer to a question then be honest and just say 'I don't know'. This is far better than trying to answer a question that you have no knowledge about. Conversely, if your answer to a question is challenged, there is nothing wrong with

sticking to your point but make sure you acknowledge the interviewer's thoughts or views. Be polite and never get into a debate.

- When you walk into the interview room stand up straight and introduce yourself. Be polite and courteous at all times and try to come across in a pleasant manner. The panel will be assessing you as soon as you walk through the door so make sure you make a positive first impression.

- Do not sit down in the interview chair until you are invited to do so. This is good manners.

- When you sit down in the interview chair, sit upright and do not fidget or slouch. It is acceptable to use hand gestures when explaining your responses to the questions but don't over do it, as this can become a distraction.

- Structure your responses to the questions in a logical manner – this is very important. When responding to an interview question start at the beginning and work your way through in a concise manner, and at a pace that is easy for the panel to listen to.

- Speak clearly and at a tone that is easy for the panel to hear. Be confident in your responses.

- When talking to the panel use eye contact but be careful not to look at them in an intimidating manner.

- Consider wearing some form of formal outfit to the interview such as a suit. Whilst you will not be assessed on the type of outfit you wear to the interview, it will make you come across in a more professional manner. Remember that you are applying to join a uniformed service.

CHAPTER EIGHT
THE PARAMEDIC SCIENCE DEGREE INTERVIEW

Students who wish to enrol on a paramedic science degree course will be required to pass a selection process that includes a numeracy and literacy test, a fitness test and an interview.

The sample numerical reasoning and verbal reasoning tests that are contained within this guide are a useful preparation aid for the tests. In relation to the fitness test, candidates are usually required to undertake the multi-stage fitness test, or bleep test, as it is otherwise known. By following the guidance that is contained within your free 'How to get paramedic fit' guide, you should be able to pass the test with relative ease.

It is the interview that the majority of candidates are concerned with, as they need to successfully convince the panel that they should choose them to embark on the paramedic science degree course.

The interview panel will normally consist of a university course tutor and a paramedic. The member of the panel who is from the university will be primarily interested in assessing whether or not you have the ability to successfully pass the course, while the paramedic will be more concerned with whether or not you possess the right skills to become a paramedic.

In the build up to the paramedic science degree interview you should concentrate your preparation on the following main areas:

- Preparing answers to the interview questions in Chapter 7.

- How you would react to certain emergency incidents.

- The role of a paramedic and the ambulance service.

- Why you want to become a paramedic.

- Why you think you can successfully pass the course.

- Issues that are affecting the NHS and the ambulance service at that particular time.

In order to help you prepare more effectively, we will now take a look at each area in detail and, more importantly, the reasons why the panel want to know this information.

HOW YOU WOULD REACT TO CERTAIN EMERGENCY INCIDENTS

As you can imagine, part of the role of the paramedic is having the ability to remain calm during extremely testing incidents. The interview panel, especially the paramedic, will be interested to see how you react to certain emergency incidents.

SCENARIO 2

As a paramedic you receive a 999 call to an incident at a nightclub. A man has been attacked and his attacker has left the scene. What would you do?

Things to consider:

- One of the first priorities, in addition to patient care, would be to request the attendance of the police. They would need to attend in order to gather details of the alleged attack and also to provide you with support and protection whilst you treat the injured.

- Again, you would need to carry out a dynamic risk assessment of the scene to ensure that you are safe.

- At all times you must remain calm. During incidents where alcohol is involved, those under the influence may act in an aggressive, violent or confrontational manner and you would need to ensure that your exit is maintained at all times.

- During incidents of this nature you may also be required to calm people down and create space so that you can attend to the casualty. During such incidents onlookers tend to gather, which can impede your ability as a paramedic to treat the patient.

The role of a paramedic and the Ambulance Service

During this guide you will have read and absorbed a large amount of information that is relevant to the role of a paramedic and the ambulance service. This information will be sufficient to prepare you for job-related questions that may come up during the paramedic science degree interview.

The majority of students who apply to become a paramedic will have hopefully never witnessed a fatality, so therefore they will need to provide an explanation of how they believe they would act in such a situation.

When preparing for this type of question think about how you would react in any of the following scenarios:

SCENARIO 1

How do you think you would react if you were the first person to arrive at the scene of a serious road traffic collision?

Things to consider:

- It is important that paramedics remain calm at all times whilst attending emergency incidents. If they are calm then they are in control and they will therefore be able to perform their duties competently and professionally.

- Whilst attending road traffic collisions paramedics and other members of the emergency services need to carry out a 'dynamic risk assessment' (DRA). In basic terms, the DRA is the management of risk through a continuous process of identifying hazards, assessing risks, taking action to eliminate or reduce risk, monitoring and reviewing, all in the rapidly changing circumstances of the operational incident. It is their responsibility to ensure that they and other people at the scene are safe.

- Patient care is vitally important. Assessing the needs of each of the casualties and providing the appropria level of care would be the task of the paramedic.

Things to consider:

- Take a look at the website of the ambulance service or NHS trust that you are interested in joining if you successfully pass the paramedic science degree course. What does it say about the role and what does it say about the ambulance service.

- Consider learning the vision and the values of the service. The panel will be impressed if you are able to recite these.

- Try to arrange a visit at your local ambulance station and ask the paramedics about their role and what it involves.

Why you want to become a paramedic

Only you will know the reason why you want to become a paramedic. When considering your response to questions based around this theme, try to think about the qualities of a paramedic that you are able to match. Keep away from reasons such as salary, pension and the opportunity to drive around in an ambulance with the blue lights flashing!

Things to consider:

The positive aspects of the role include:

- The chance to make a difference.

- Working with a highly professional team of people.

- The opportunity to work within a diverse workforce and a diverse community.

- Learning new skills and obtaining qualifications.

- Working in a job where no two days are the same – the variety of the job.

Why you think you can successfully pass the course

Those candidates who can demonstrate they have previous history of successfully completing difficult tasks and training courses are far more likely to stick with the degree course and pass it.

During the interview the panel may ask you to explain why you think you can successfully pass the paramedic science degree course. During your response it is important that you can provide details of where you have previously worked hard in order to gain a qualification or complete a training course. You will most probably have studied hard previously to pass either your GCSEs or A-Levels and this evidence should form the basis of your response.

The panel will also want to see a demonstration of enthusiasm and passion from you, as this will provide further evidence of your commitment to successfully completing the course.

Questions of this nature are usually designed to separate those candidates who are genuinely interested and passionate about becoming a paramedic from those who are simply going through the motions and have not put any real thought into their chosen course or career path.

Things to consider:

- Provide details of where you have previously studied over a long period of time and obtained some form of qualification.

- Demonstrate a level of passion and enthusiasm for the course and for the role of a paramedic.

- Provide evidence of where you have gone out of your way to find out about the course and also the role of a paramedic.

Issues that are affecting the NHS and the ambulance service at that particular time

At any particular time there will be certain issues affecting the NHS. For example, at the time of writing this guide one of the most important issues affecting the NHS is that of 'swine flu' and how the government and the NHS aim to tackle the problem and prevent its spread.

The reason why the panel ask this type of question is to assess whether or not you have a genuine interest in the NHS and the Ambulance Service.

Make sure you keep up to date with current affairs that are affecting the NHS, the role of a paramedic and the Ambulance Service.

Things to consider

- In the build up to your interview visit websites and chat forums on the internet to learn what the current topical issues are that are affecting the NHS.

- Consider subscribing to a paramedic journal or magazine, as these will usually contain up-to-date issues and current affairs.

CHAPTER NINE
FREE HOW TO GET PARAMEDIC FIT GUIDE

On the following pages I have created for you a free 'How to get Paramedic Fit' information guide. This guide has been designed to help you prepare for and pass the occupational fitness test that forms part of the paramedic and emergency care assistant selection process. It contains a variety of useful exercises and fitness programmes to help you get, and stay, paramedic fit.

During your fitness preparation, try to think about the role of the paramedic. What type of physical activity do they undertake during their everyday work? Climbing stairs with heavy equipment and performing cardiac massage for potentially prolonged periods are just two areas. Now try to think of the types of exercises that will help you prepare for this work – step-ups, walking, jogging, squats and rowing.

The most effective way to prepare for the fitness test is to

embark on a structured fitness programme that is based around the above exercises.

As with any fitness training programme, it is important that you consult your GP before carrying out any form of physical exercise.

In order for paramedics to perform their normal medical duties whilst wearing personal protective equipment (PPE), they need to maintain a reasonable level of physical fitness. The Ambulance Service need to satisfy themselves that you are already at the minimum standard of fitness and that you are also capable of maintaining this level throughout your career. Each NHS trust will vary in terms of its selection process. However, the majority of them will require you to pass an occupational fitness test and a lifting and handling ability test.

As an example, some Ambulance Services require you to pair up with another candidate and carry a 48kg dummy placed in a carry chair up and down a short flight of stairs. During this test you must ensure that you utilise correct lifting technique, i.e. back straight, look up and bend knees etc.

This form of assessment will also demonstrate your grip and overall body strength. An instructor will demonstrate the techniques involved before you are requested to perform the lift and carry.

On the following pages I have provided you with information relating to Paramedic Science Degree fitness test and also manual handling techniques. I strongly advise that you confirm that the following information is accurate, and that you are fit and healthy, before carrying out any form of heavy lifting.

AMBULANCE SERVICE NHS TRUST PARAMEDIC SCIENCE DEGREE FITNESS TEST

As part of the selection process for the BSc (Hons) Paramedic Science degree you may be required to complete a fitness test. The test is designed to assess your ability to carry out peak demands of ambulance work. SECAmb feels that this is necessary to ensure that you have sufficient physical ability to cope with extreme work demands, as and when these occur, and to minimise the health/injury risks known to exist within low fitness groups when regularly engaged in such hard physical work.

The testing objectives include being able to determine heart, lung and blood vessel capacities for whole body activity, muscular strength, flexibility and body composition. If you have not engaged in physical activity for some time, are not used to exercise, or suspect any problems (e.g. heart, joint or muscle) that may be made worse by exercise, please consult your own GP. The test, that should last no longer than 20 minutes in total, is physically demanding and you need to be medically fit to undertake it.

PREPARING FOR THE TEST

It is suggested you consult your GP before starting any exercise programme, especially if you have not engaged in physical activity for some time, are not used to exercise, or suspect any problems (e.g. heart, joint, or muscle), that may be made worse by exercise. Do not exercise if you have, or are recovering from colds, flu, fever, etc. If you require any further advice about types of exercise, intensities or duration, seek the assistance of a reputable qualified fitness trainer or health club, explaining your requirements.

GRIP STRENGTH:
Perform these exercises at regular intervals throughout the day.

1. Squeezing a stress ball

2. Use spring loaded grip handles

3. Squeezing a tennis ball

BACK STRENGTH:
Perform these exercises at regular intervals throughout the day.

1. Swimming.

2. Back raises

3 sets of 10 reps:

*   Lie flat on the floor and raise just the upper body 6-8 inches off the floor.

*   Keep legs straight and both feet on the floor at all times.

AEROBIC EXERCISES:
20-40 minutes every other day.

1. Running.

2. Walking up and down stairs.

3. Use a rowing machine.

4. Cycling or cycle machine.

ADDITIONAL ADVICE:

To help with all exercises do 3 sets of 10 reps of the following:

Upper body exercises:	**Lower body exercises:**
Dumbbell curls	Leg extensions
Tricep dips	Hamstring curls
Press ups	Leg press
Sit ups	Squats
Lunges	

Alternatively join a gym, explain to the personal trainer what you need to achieve, and take their advice. If while doing any of the above exercises you experience any pain, discomfort or difficulty breathing, stop immediately and consult your GP.

THE FITNESS TEST

The test will comprise of a number of elements each of which is listed below.

Fitness test elements

1. Aerobic capacity

The test will consist of a one minute period stepping up and down a 30cm step in time to a metronome. Following this period the candidate will commence one minute of chest compressions on a manikin.

The candidates heart rate will be measured during the period of activity and then for a period of 2 minutes after exercise to measure recovery heart rates.

The candidate will be wearing a heart rate monitor throughout this test and the readings will be taken at 30 second intervals.

The candidate will be measured against the following outcomes:

a. Maximal heart rate – the candidate should not exceed 90% of maximum heart rate value. This is calculated by the formula

$$(220 - age) \times 0.9$$

If the candidates heart rate exceeds this value during exercise and looks as if the exercise is having a negative impact on the candidate the test will be stopped.

b. Following exercise the candidate's heart rate should fall. We would expect to see the heart rate fall by 12 beats a minute over the 2 minute period. If this fails to happen the candidate will not pass the aerobic assessment and will be advised to seek further assessment from a Doctor.

c. Following exercise the candidate's heart rate should fall below 120 beats per minute by the end of the 2 minute recovery period. If this fails to happen the candidate will not pass the assessment and will be advised to seek further assessment from a Doctor.

2. Back Strength

The candidate will be tested on lower back strength. The candidate will be expected to achieve a pull of 100 kg. The test will be completed on a machine as shown below:

The candidate will be instructed in safe use of the machine and correct technique before they are asked to complete the assessment. The candidate will be given 2 opportunities to achieve the outcome.

3. Grip strength

The candidate will be tested on grip strength in both hands. The candidate has to achieve grip strength of 31kg in their dominant hand and 30 kg in their non-dominant hand. The test will be completed using the machine shown below:

The candidate will be instructed in safe use of the machine and correct technique before they are asked to complete the assessment. The candidate will be given 3 opportunities to achieve the outcome.

4. Flexibility

The candidate will be tested on hamstring / lower back flexibility. The test will comprise of the candidate sitting on the floor, legs straight and being asked to touch their toes. The candidate will be instructed on how to safely complete this assessment.

All tests will be overseen by a qualified instructor. The candidates will be asked to sign a disclaimer before the fitness assessments are carried out and the candidates must declare any physical / fitness problems prior to participation. The tests can be halted at the instructor's discretion if they feel the assessments are having a negative impact of the candidate's health.

The candidates are asked to bring / wear suitable clothing to this assessment and flat shoes. The test will not be completed if the candidate is not wearing appropriate footwear.

A candidate has to pass all elements of the fitness assessment in order to progress.

MANUAL HANDLING TECHNIQUES

Correct lifting techniques are very important. During your training to become a paramedic you will undertake a comprehensive manual handling training course. However, before you go through selection it is a good idea to familiarise yourself with some of the more safety-critical aspects of manual handling and lifting.

Remember:

- Many hands make light work – never try to lift anything that is too heavy on your own. Look for advice labels and instructions on heavy and awkward objects.

- Check the route you have to cover before you start carrying objects. You don't want to have to stop unnecessarily to get around objects or obstructions.

Before you lift anything:

- Check how heavy it is.

- Are there bits that could fall off?

- Can you wheel it?

- Has it got handles? If so use them.

- Do you need help to carry it? Never be ashamed to ask for help.

- If more than one of you is lifting it, establish who will be in charge, to ensure that you work as a team.

9 KEY SAFETY POINTS FOR MANUAL HANDLING

Before lifting heavy items of equipment it is advisable that you:

1. Think before you lift and handle the object – where are you going to take it and what route will you take? Is the route clear from obstructions?

2. How heavy is the object and can it be lifted by an alternative means such as lifting equipment? Do you need to get assistance? If there is no other alternative other than to manually lift the object, how will you lift it off the floor? Are there any carrying handles and is there any safety information provided on the object?

3. Ensure your position is stable – by keeping your feet apart with one leg slightly forward, you will be able to maintain balance. Your feet should be moved to maintain balance during the lift. Avoid tight clothing and unsuitable footwear, which might impair movement. Keep and maintain good posture – at the start of the lift, slight bending of the back, hips and knees is preferable to fully flexing the back (stooping) or fully flexing the hips or knees (squatting).

4. Hold the load securely and maintain a good grip whilst lifting.

5. Keep looking forward in the direction you are travelling. Do not look down but make sure your route is safe and free from trip hazards and obstructions.

6. Keep your knees slightly bent, as this will allow you to absorb some of the load through your legs.

7. Avoid any unnecessary flexing or twisting of the back whilst lifting. You should also avoid leaning sideways. All of these can lead to injury. Your shoulders should be level and facing the same direction as the hips. Turning by moving the feet is better than twisting and lifting at the same time. Keep your elbows slightly bent and ensure you have a secure grip on the object.

8. Hold the object close to your body.

9. Make sure the object does not obstruct your vision and your direction of travel. You must be able to see your route and able to notice any obstructions or trip hazards.

HOW TO IMPROVE YOUR STAMINA FOR THE LIFTING AND HANDLING ABILITY TEST

The most effective method for increasing your strength is to perform exercises that involve the use of your legs. This may involve squats, leg extensions, rowing, running, brisk walking, swimming or other similar exercises.

Only you know your own abilities and strengths and it is up to you to assess your weaknesses and make a plan to improve them.

Within this guide I have provided some exercises, which have all been designed to help you improve your overall fitness and stamina.

OCCUPATIONAL FITNESS TEST

The selection process for qualified paramedics, emergency care assistants and student paramedics may include a physical capability test. This will not apply to every NHS trust but you will be advised in your application pack of the required standard if this applies to the service you are attempting to join.

The test is a sub-maximal occupational fitness test. It is designed to assess ability to carry out peak demands of ambulance work. This is necessary to ensure that you have sufficient physical ability to cope with extreme work demands, as and when these occur.

The type of work you will be required to do during peak demands will involve the climbing of stairs, carrying equipment and performing cardiac massage for a protracted length of time.

In order to assess your capability and fitness to perform these tasks, the test will involve a number of stages of stepping on and off 15cm and 30cm height steps at varying stepping speeds.

This stage of the test normally lasts no longer than 20 minutes. Some stages include carrying weighted equipment up to 30kg, and one stage requires the application of cardiac massage to a resuscitation doll (training in technique will be given beforehand).

If you feel that your current fitness level may handicap your ability to complete such an assessment, follow the advice given below. In order to assist your preparation, it is recommended that you start and follow a regular programme of fitness training, which should commence some months before attempting the selection test.

Any exercise that is continuous, rhythmical, and engages the large muscle groups of the body, would be suitable.

Typical activities would include:

- Walking or jogging;
- Cycling;
- Rowing;
- Swimming;
- Step/circuit training.

The exercise should not cause exhaustion or leave you totally breathless. On the following pages I have provided you with a selection of exercises to assist you during your preparation.

Read the guide, assess your own level of fitness, and choose a number of training programmes/exercises that are suitable for your own individual needs.

PLANNING YOUR WORKOUTS AND PREPARING FOR THE OCCUPATIONAL FITNESS TEST

Most people who embark on a fitness regime in January have given it up by February. The reason why most people give up their fitness regime so soon is mainly due to a lack of proper preparation. You will recall that throughout the duration of this guide the word preparation has been integral, and the same word applies when preparing for the occupational fitness tests for becoming a paramedic or emergency care assistant. Preparation is key to your success and it is essential that you plan your workouts effectively.

In the build up to the occupational physical tests I advise that you concentrate on specific exercises that will allow you to pass the tests with ease. Read on for some great ways to pass the tests and stay fit all year round.

Get an assessment before you start training

The first step is to get a fitness test at the gym, weigh yourself and run your fastest mile. Once you have done all three of these you should write down your results and keep them hidden away somewhere safe. After a month of following your new fitness regime, do all three tests again and check your results against the previous months. This is a great way to monitor your performance and progress and it will also keep you motivated and focused on your goals.

Keep a check on what you eat and drink.

Make sure you write down everything you eat and drink for a whole week. You must include tea, water, milk, biscuits and anything and everything that you digest. You will soon begin to realise how much you are eating and you will notice areas in which you can make some changes. For example, if you are taking sugar with your tea then why not try reducing it or

giving it up all together. If you do then you will soon notice the difference.

It is important that you start to look for opportunities to improve your fitness and well-being right from the offset. These areas are what I call 'easy wins'.

Exercises that will help you to pass the fitness tests

It is my strong belief that you do not have to attend a gym in order to prepare for the occupational fitness tests. If I was applying to become a paramedic today then I would embark on a fitness programme that included brisk walking, running, rowing, presses, step ups, squats and lunges. In order to improve my upper body strength I would also go swimming and carry out lengths of breast stroke – this is great exercise for the simulated cardiac massage assessment.

In addition to swimming, fast walking is one of the best exercises you can do as part of your preparation for the occupational fitness tests. Whilst it shouldn't be the only form of exercise you carry out, it will go along way to improving your focus and general well being. Try walking at a fast pace for 30 minutes every day for a 7 day period. Then see how you feel at the end of the 7 day period. I guarantee you'll begin to feel a lot healthier and fitter. Fast walking is also a fantastic way to lose weight if you think you need to. In addition to helping you to lose weight it will also keep your concentration and motivational levels up.

There are some more great exercises contained within this guide and most of them can be carried out without the need to attend a gym.

One step at a time

Only you will know how fit you are. I advise that you first of all write down the areas that you believe or feel you need

to improve on. For example, if you feel that you need to work on your upper body strength in order to pass the lifting and simulated cardiac massage assessment then pick out exercises from this guide that will work on that area for you.

The key to making improvements is to do it gradually, and at one step at a time. Try to set yourself small goals. If you think you need to lose two stone in weight then focus on losing a few pounds at a time. For example, during the first month aim to lose 6 pounds only. Once you have achieved this then again aim to lose 6 pounds over the next month, and so on and so forth. The more realistic your goal, the more likely you are to achieve it. One of the biggest problems that people encounter when starting a fitness regime is they become bored quickly. This then leads to a lack of motivation and desire, and soon the fitness programme stops.

Change your exercise routine often. Instead of swimming try jogging. Instead of jogging try cycling with the odd day of rowing. Keep your workouts varied and interesting to ensure that you stay focused and motivated.

STRETCHING

How many people stretch before carrying out any form of exercise? Very few people is the correct answer. Not only is it irresponsible but it is also placing yourself at high risk from injury. Before we commence with the exercises we will take a look at a few warm up stretches. Make sure you stretch fully before carrying out any exercises. You want your paramedic career to be a long one and that means looking after yourself, including stretching! It is also very important to check with your GP that you are medically fit to carry out any form of physical exercise.

The warm-up calf stretch

To perform this stretch effectively you should first of all start off by facing a wall whilst standing upright. Your right foot should be close to the wall and your right knee bent. Now place your hands flat against the wall and at a height that is level with your shoulders. Stretch your left leg far out behind you without lifting your toes and heel off the floor, and lean towards the wall.

Once you have performed this stretch for 25 seconds switch legs and carry out the same procedure for the left leg. As with all exercises contained within this guide, stop if you feel any pain or discomfort.

Stretching the shoulder muscles

To begin with, stand with your feet slightly apart and with your knees only slightly bent. Now hold your arms right out in front of you and with your palms facing away from you with your fingers pointing skywards. Now place your right palm on the back of your left hand and use it to push the left hand further away from you. If you are performing this exercise correctly then you will feel the muscles in your shoulder stretching. Hold for 10 seconds before switching sides.

Stretching the quad muscles (front of the thigh)

Before you carry out any form of brisk walking or running then it is imperative that you stretch your leg muscles.

To begin with, stand with your right hand pressed against the back of a wall or firm surface. Bend your left knee and bring your left heel up to your bottom whilst grasping your foot with your left hand. Your back should be straight and your shoulders, hips and knees should all be in line at all times during the exercise. Hold for 25 seconds before switching legs.

Stretching the hamstring muscles (back of the thigh)

To perform this exercise correctly, stand up straight and place your right foot onto a table or other firm surface so that your leg is almost parallel to the floor. Keep your left leg straight and your foot at a right angle to your leg. Start to slowly move your hands down your right leg towards your ankle until you feel tension on the underside of your thigh. When you feel this tension you know that you are starting to stretch the hamstring muscles. Hold for 25 seconds before switching legs.

We have only covered a small number of stretching exercises within this section; however, it is crucial that you stretch out fully in all areas before carrying out any of the following exercises. Remember to obtain professional advice before carrying out type of exercise.

RUNNING

One of the great ways to prepare for the occupational fitness tests is to embark on a structured running programme. You do not need to run at a fast pace, or even run for long distances, in order to gain massively from this type of exercise. Before I provide you with a sample running programme, however, take a read of the following important tips.

Tips for running:

- As with any exercise you should consult a doctor before taking part to make sure that you are medically fit.

- It is certainly worth investing in a pair of comfortable running shoes that serve the purpose for your intended training programme. Your local sports shop will be able to advise you on the type that is best for you. You don't

have to spend a fortune to buy a good pair of running shoes.

- It is a good idea to invest in a 'high visibility' jacket or coat so that you can be seen by fast moving traffic if you intend to run on or near the road.

- Make sure you carry out at least 5 whole minutes of stretching exercise not only before but also after your running programme. This can help to prevent injury.

- Whilst you shouldn't run on a full stomach, it is also not good to run on an empty one either. A great food to eat approximately 30 minutes before a run is a banana. This is great for giving you energy.

- Drink plenty of water throughout the day. Try to drink at least 1.5 litres each day in total. This will keep you hydrated and help to prevent muscle cramp.

- Don't overdo it. If you feel any pain or discomfort then stop and seek medical advice.

RUNNING PROGRAMME WEEK 1

DAY 1

- Run a total of 3 miles only.

If you cannot manage 3 miles then try the following:

- Walk at a brisk pace for half a mile or approximately 10 minutes.

Then

- Run for 1 mile or 8 minutes.

Then

- Walk for another half a mile or approximately 10 minutes.

Then

- Run for 1.5 miles or 12 minutes.

Walking at a brisk pace is possibly the most effective way to lose weight if you need to. It is possible to burn the same amount of calories if you walk the same distance as if you were running.

When walking at a 'brisk' pace it is recommended that you walk as fast as is comfortably possible without breaking into a run or slow jog.

DAY 2

- Walk for 2 miles or approximately 20 minutes at a brisk pace.

Then

- Run for 2 miles or 14 minutes.

DAY 3

- Repeat DAY ONE.

DAY 4

- Walk at a brisk pace for 0.5 miles or approximately 7 minutes.

Then

- Run for 3 miles or 20 minutes.

DAY 5

- Repeat day one.

DAY 6 AND DAY 7

- Rest days. No exercise.

RUNNING PROGRAMME WEEK 2

DAY 1

- Run for 4 miles or 25 minutes.

DAY 2

- Run a total of 3 miles only.

If you cannot manage 3 miles then try the following:

- Walk at a brisk pace for half a mile or approximately 10 minutes.

Then

- Run for 1 mile or 8 minutes.

Then

- Walk for another half a mile or approximately 10 minutes.

Then

- Run for 1.5 miles or 12 minutes.

DAY 3

- Rest day. No exercise.

DAY 4

- Run for 5 miles or 35 minutes.

DAY 5

- Run for 3 miles or 20 minutes.

Then

- Walk at a brisk pace for 2 miles or approximately 20 minutes.

DAY 6

- Run for 5 miles or 35 minutes.

DAY 7

- Rest day. No exercise.

EXERCISES

Press-ups

Whilst running is a great way to improve your overall fitness, you will also need to carry out exercises that improve your upper body strength. These exercises will help you to pass the lifting and handling ability test, which may form part of the fitness tests. This type of exercise is also ideal for the simulated cardiac massage assessment (if applicable).

The great thing about press-ups is that you don't have to attend a gym to perform them. However, you must ensure that you can do them correctly as injury can occur.

You may wish to spend just 5 minutes every day on press-ups, possibly after you go running or even before if you prefer. If you are not used to doing press-ups then start slowly and aim to carry out at least 10.

Even if you struggle to do just 10, you will soon find that after a few days practice at these you will be up to 20+.

WARNING – Ensure you take advice from a competent fitness trainer in relation to the correct execution of press-up exercises.

Step 1 – To begin with, lie on a mat or even surface. Your hands should be shoulder width apart & fully extend the arms.

Step 2 – Gradually lower your body until the elbows reach 90°. Do not rush the movement as you may cause injury.

Step 3 – Once your elbows reach 90° slowly return to the starting position with your arms fully extended.

The press up action should be a continuous movement with no rest. However, it is important that the exercise is as smooth as possible and there should be no jolting or sudden movements. Try to complete as many press ups as possible and always keep a record of how many you do. This will keep your focus and also maintain your motivation levels.

Sit-ups

Sit ups are great for building the core stomach muscles. At the commencement of the exercise lie flat on your back with your knees bent at a 45° angle and with your feet together. Your hands can either be crossed on your chest, by your sides, or cupped behind your ears as indicated in the diagram below.

Without moving your lower body, curl your upper torso upwards and in towards your knees, until your shoulder blades are as high off the ground as possible. As you reach the highest point, tighten your abdominals muscles for a brief second. This will allow you to get the most out of the exercise. Now slowly start to lower yourself back to the starting position. You should be aiming to work up to at least 50 effective sit-ups every day. You will be amazed at how

quickly this can be achieved and you will begin to notice your stomach muscles developing.

Whilst sit-ups do not form part of occupational fitness tests, they are still a great way of improving your all-round fitness and therefore should not be neglected.

Pull ups

Pull ups are another great way for building the core upper body muscle groups. The unfortunate thing about this type of exercise is you will probably need to attend a gym in order to carry them out. Having said that, there are a number of different types of 'pull up bars' available to buy on the market that can easily and safely be fitted to a doorway at home. If you choose to purchase one of these items make sure that it conforms to the relevant safety standards first.

Lateral pull-ups are very effective at increasing upper body strength. If you have access to a gymnasium then these can be practised on a 'lateral pull-down' machine. It is advised that you consult your gym member of staff to ask about these exercises.

Pull ups should be performed by

grasping firmly a sturdy and solid bar. Before you grasp the bar make sure it is safe. Your hands should be roughly shoulder width apart. Straighten your arms so that your body hangs loose. You will feel your lateral muscles and biceps stretching as you hang in the air. This is the starting position for the lateral pull up exercise.

Next, pull yourself upwards to the point where your chest is almost touching the bar and your chin is actually over the bar. Whilst pulling upwards, focus on keeping your body straight without any arching or swinging as this can result in injury. Once your chin is over the bar, you can lower yourself back down to the initial starting position. Repeat the exercise 10 times.

Squats (these work the legs and bottom)

Squats are a great exercise for working the leg muscles. They are the perfect exercise in your preparation for the occupational fitness tests and in particular the lifting and handling assessment (if applicable).

At the commencement of the exercise, stand up straight with your arms at your sides. Concentrate on keeping your feet shoulder-width apart and your head up. Do not look downwards at any point during the exercise. You will see from the diagram above that the person has their lower back slightly arched. They are also holding light weights which can add to the intensity of the exercise.

Now start to very slowly bend your knees while pushing your rear out as though you are about to sit down on a chair. Keep lowering yourself down until your thighs reach pas the 90° point. Make sure your weight is on your heels so that your knees do not extend over your toes. At this point you may wish to tighten your thighs and buttocks to intensify the exercise.

As you come back up to a standing position, push down through your heels which will allow you to maintain your balance. Repeat the exercise 15 to 20 times.

Lunges (these work the thighs and bottom)

You will have noticed throughout this section of the guide that I have been providing you with simple, yet highly effective exercises that can be carried out at home. The lunge exercise is another great addition to the range of exercises that require no attendance at the gym.

To begin with, stand with your back straight and your feet together (you may hold light hand weights if you wish to add some intensity to the exercise).

Next, take a big step forward as illustrated in the above diagram making sure you inhale as go and landing with the heel first. Bend the front knee no more than 90 degrees so as to avoid injury. Keep your back straight and lower the back knee as close to the floor as possible. Your

front knee should be lined up over your ankle and your back thigh should be in line with your back.

To complete the exercise, exhale and push down against your front heel, squeezing your buttocks tight as you rise back to a starting position.

Try to repeat the exercise 15 to 20 times before switching sides.

Lateral raises (these work the shoulder muscles)

Paramedics are usually required to lift heavy items of equipment during their day to day work. Lateral raises will allow you improve your upper body strength in a safe and effective manner.

Take a dumbbell in each hand and hold them by the sides of your body with the palms facing inward.

Stand or sit with your feet shoulder-width apart, knees slightly bent. Do not lean backwards as you could cause injury to your back. Raise your arms up and out to the sides until they are parallel to the ground, then lower them back down carefully. Repeat the exercise 15 to 20 times.

ALTERNATIVES EXERCISES

Swimming

Apart from press-ups, lateral raises and the other exercises I have provided you with, another fantastic way to improve your upper body and overall fitness is to go swimming. If you have access to a swimming pool, and you can swim, then this is a brilliant way to improve your fitness.

If you are not a great swimmer you can start off with short distances and gradually build up your swimming strength and stamina. Breaststroke is sufficient for building good upper body strength providing you put the effort into swimming an effective number of lengths. You may wish to alternate your running programme with the odd day of swimming. If you can swim 10 lengths of a 25-metre pool initially then this is a good base to start from. You will soon find that you can increase this number easily providing that you carry on swimming every week. Try running to your local swimming pool if it is not too far away, swimming 20 lengths of breaststroke, and then running back home.

This is a great way to combine your fitness activity and prevent yourself from becoming bored of your training programme.

Rowing

If there is one exercise that will allow you to work every single muscle group in the body then it is rowing. This is the perfect exercise for preparing to pass the occupational fitness tests. It will increase your aerobic fitness and it will also improve your lower and upper body strength.

As with any exercise of this nature there is a risk of injury. It is crucial that you use the correct technique when rowing on a purpose built machine. By applying the correct technique you will be far more efficient and you will also see faster results.

Whilst exercising on the rowing machine, make sure you keep your back straight and concentrate on using your legs and buttocks. Never extend so far that you lock out your knees. Try and be smooth throughout the entire exercise. To obtain a suitable indoor rowing training programme that is relevant to your current fitness levels please visit www.concept2.co.uk.

TIPS FOR STAYING WITH YOUR WORKOUT

The hardest part of your training programme will be sticking with it. In this final section of your fitness guide I will provide some useful golden rules that will enable you to maintain your motivational levels in the build up to the selection process. In order to stay with your workout for longer, try following these simple rules:

Golden rule number one – Work out often

Aim to train three to five times each and every week.

Each training session should last between 20 minutes to a maximum of an hour. The quality of training is important so don't go for heavy weights but instead go for a lighter weight with a better technique. On days when you are feeling energetic, take advantage of this opportunity and do more!

Within this guide I have deliberately provided you with a number of 'simple to perform' exercises that are targeted at the core muscle groups required to perform the role of a paramedic. In between your study sessions try carrying out these exercises at home or get yourself out on road running or cycling. Use your study 'down time' effectively and wisely.

Golden rule number two – Mix up your exercises

Your exercise programme should include some elements of cardiovascular (aerobics, running, brisk walking and cycling),

resistance training (weights or own body exercises such as press-ups and sit ups) and, finally, flexibility (stretching). Make sure that you always warm up and warm down.

If you are a member of a gym then consider taking up a class such as Pilates. This form of exercise class will teach you how to build core training into your exercise principles, and show you how to hit your abdominals in ways that are not possible with conventional sit-ups. If you are a member of a gym then a fantastic 'all round' exercise that I strongly recommend is rowing. Rowing will hit every major muscle group in your body and it is also perfect for improving your stamina levels and cardiovascular fitness.

Golden rule number three – Eat a healthy and balanced diet

It is vitally important that you eat the right fuel to give you the energy to train to your full potential. Don't fill your body with rubbish and then expect to train well. Think about what you are eating and drinking, including the quantities, and keep a record of what you are digesting. You will become stronger and fitter more quickly if you eat little amounts of nutritious foods at short intervals.

Golden rule number four – Get help

Try working with a personal trainer. They will ensure that you work hard and will help you to achieve your goals. If you cannot afford a personal trainer then try training with someone else. The mere fact that they are there at your side will add an element of competition to your training sessions!

A consultation with a professional nutritionist will also help you improve your eating habits and establish your individual food needs.

Golden rule number five – Fitness is for life

One of my old managers in the Fire Service had a saying – "Fitness Wins!" Two simple words, that meant an awful lot. Improving your fitness and eating healthily are not short-term projects. They are things that should come naturally to you.

Make fitness a permanent part of your life by following these tips, and you'll lead a better and more fulfilling life!

Good luck and work hard to improve your weak areas.

A FEW FINAL WORDS

You have now reached the end of the guide and no doubt you will be ready to start preparing for the paramedic/emergency care assistant selection process. Just before you go off and start on your preparation, consider the following.

The majority of candidates who pass the selection process have a number of common attributes. These are as follows:

1. They believe in themselves.

The first factor is self-belief. Regardless of what anyone tells you, you can become a paramedic. Just like any job of this nature, you have to be prepared to work hard in order to be successful. Make sure you have the self-belief to pass the selection process and fill your mind with positive thoughts.

2. They prepare fully.

The second factor is preparation. Those people who achieve in life prepare fully for every eventuality and that is what you must do when you apply to become a paramedic. Work very hard and especially concentrate on your weak areas.

3. They persevere.

Perseverance is a fantastic word. Everybody comes across obstacles or setbacks in their life, but it is what you do about those setbacks that is important. If you fail at something, then ask yourself 'why' you have failed. This will allow you to improve for next time and if you keep improving and trying, success will eventually follow. Apply this same method of thinking when you apply to become a paramedic.

4. They are self-motivated.

How much do you want this job? Do you want it, or do you really want it?

When you apply to join the Ambulance Service you should want it more than anything in the world. You levels of self-motivation will shine through on your application and during your interview. For the weeks and months leading up to the paramedic selection process, be motivated as best you can and always keep your fitness levels up as this will serve to increase your levels of motivation.

Work hard, stay focused and be what you want...

Richard McMunn

Attend a 1-Day
Paramedic Training
Course at

www.ParamedicCourse.co.uk